PRAISE FOR

The Art of Teaching Art to Children

"What an invaluable treasure for educators, parents, or for that matter, anyone who works with children! The wisdom of this book goes far beyond teaching art. With her developmentally appropriate approach to teaching children, Beal outlines a way of teaching that can be transposed to any educational situation. It is an indispensable reference for schools, homes, and libraries that is sure to become a classic."

—Jeff Wallis, Principal, Dwight-Englewood
Lower School, Englewood, New Jersey

"This is a gem of a book!"

—Janie Lou Hirsch, Director, Westland School,
Los Angeles

"Nancy Beal's work is grounded in her having thoughtfully reflected on years of teaching experience with young children. This book will become a standard for any elementary art teacher as well as a useful guide for parents who want to encourage their children's art."

—Elizabeth Larkin, Assistant Professor of Education,
University of South Florida

THE ART
OF TEACHING ART
TO CHILDREN

THE ART
OF TEACHING ART
TO CHILDREN

In School and at Home

NANCY BEAL

with Gloria Bley Miller

FARRAR, STRAUS AND GIROUX

New York

Farrar, Straus and Giroux
19 Union Square West, New York 10003

Copyright © 2001 by Nancy Beal and Gloria Bley Miller
All rights reserved
Distributed in Canada by Douglas & McIntyre Ltd.
Printed in the United States of America
First edition, 2001

The photographs on the following pages are by Lilyan Aloma: 31, 32, 33, 38, 120, 126, 127, 128, 132, 133, 167, 170, 171, 172, 173, 177, 179, 180, 181, 184, 201, 203, 205, 207. The photographs of the children are by Nancy Beal.

Library of Congress Cataloging-in-Publication Data
Beal, Nancy, 1942–
    The art of teaching art to children : in school and at home / Nancy Beal,
  with Gloria Bley Miller.— 1st ed.
      p. cm.
    Includes bibliographical references and index.
    ISBN-13: 978-0-374-52770-9
    ISBN-10: 0-374-52770-9 (pb : alk. paper)
    1. Art—Study and teaching (Elementary)   I. Miller, Gloria Bley. II. Title.

N350 .B37 2001
372.5'044—dc21

2001018759

Designed by Jonathan D. Lippincott

www.fsgbooks.com

13 12 11 10 9 8 7 6 5

To Lois Lord,
who has taught me
what is important
in teaching art

CONTENTS

Preface

Young children learn by re-creating their own experience. Building with blocks, they create a model of the world they know to better comprehend that world. Through dramatic play, they explore family relationships. By reconstructing their own lives, they try to sort out the significance of what is happening in the fresh, new world around them.

Art, like play, helps children to understand their world. But art goes beyond play, enabling them to express their personal experiences and fantasies in ways that are concrete and compelling, even when they are unable to articulate the events in words.

Children love to make direct physical contact with their universe. Art invites them to touch and experiment, to explore and transform. Most significantly, it allows them to visualize, to make the intangible concrete. When they are able to pin something down, they know they own it.

With the younger children, their subject matter is the art materials themselves. As they get older, they begin to master those materials and to become more focused and controlled.

Their subject matter starts to grow out of their own life experiences, their personal concerns, and their rich imaginations. To convey an idea, they may draw it, paint it, or model it in clay. To create their images, they will use shapes, lines, colors, movement, textures, and so on.

Flexible art materials offer the children infinite opportunities to express themselves. The teacher sets these materials out, then asks some key questions to engage the children's hearts and minds. The starting point is the word *how*, which embodies both a challenge and a license. The teacher asks, "How would you like to put these colors together?" "How can you build in clay?" "How can you show a time when you're having a party?"

The word *how* is used here in an entirely different manner than in the typical "how-to" approach of most art teaching, which sets up certain specific projects with foregone conclusions and almost preordained results. The how takes on a whole new meaning here, welcoming the children into the realm of freedom. They are free to make choices, to do it their way, to develop their preferences. They are free to create their own clarity and order through art.

In effect, the children are stating how they themselves want to approach their work, bringing their own personal responses to the questions the teacher has raised. And the teacher—by accepting what they are doing—reaffirms their individuality and their right to express their personal viewpoints. Because their unique form of expression has been validated and valued, the children begin to feel confident about themselves. They learn to respect their own work and the work of others. And they begin to be open to all kinds of learning.

Art, in short, is extremely important to the children's development and helps them become more imaginative and responsive adults. Considering the time they spend sitting in front of computer (and television) screens today, the hands-on experience that art offers has become more important than ever.

Art is indeed a major language of childhood. And that language is spoken very well, here in this book.

—Gloria Bley Miller

Acknowledgments

In addition to dedicating this book to Lois Lord, my teacher and friend, who shared with me her wisdom about art and children and the understanding she developed with her colleagues, especially Nancy Smith, I would like to thank the following:

Sheila Emerson Sadler, founding director of the Village Community School, where I teach. I owe much to her vision of a school where everyone—teachers and students alike—can be and can do their very best.

Sari Grossman, who is outstanding in her ability to match learning, which is age-appropriate and hands-on, with an in-depth social studies curriculum. (I also want to thank all my other colleagues at the school who have shared their insights about children with me.)

Ann Schaumberger, my close friend and a fellow artist, who, like me, teaches art to children, and with whom I have enjoyed many enriching conversations about our mutual profession.

My parents, William G. Beal and Cynthia Cate Beal. My father's enthusiasm for children has always been contagious, while the hand-and-eye skills my mother taught me in childhood are the things I find so useful in teaching today.

My husband, Michael Mostow, and my daughter, Sarah Cate Mostow. Michael's steady support has been unfailing in all ways, while Sarah has shared with me her love of art and art history, as well as her great enthusiasm for this book.

Gloria Bley Miller, who encouraged me to do this book in the first place, then participated in every phase of its development and helped me keep the text eminently readable.

And finally, my wonderful students at the Village Community School, who have delighted me over the years with their eagerness, their interest, and their remarkable vitality.

Introduction

After graduating from college with a major in painting and a minor in education, I started working in elementary schools, teaching the usual subjects: reading, writing, arithmetic, and social studies. I taught out on Long Island and at the Friends Seminary in Manhattan. When I heard about the Village Community School, I applied for employment there and was hired to teach the nine- and ten-year-olds. After a few years of classroom teaching at that school, I felt I wanted something more. I wanted to teach art, even though I hadn't been trained for it. Because I had studied art and did exhibit my paintings professionally, the school gave me one day a week; later it became two days and, finally, it was full-time.

But I did not know how one goes about teaching art to children. For many years, I was terrible at it. I didn't understand that the world of art has a different meaning for children; that for them, art is about *their* life experiences.

Some teachers may take a characteristic of modern art that is simple to convey and have the children play with it visually. These teachers start with an adult concept by an adult artist. I did that myself. I remember drumming up a project that I thought would be good for kids of about ten. The goal was to do an abstract painting. (I don't paint abstractly myself, but I was sure it would look good.) I had the kids cut a small rectangle, like a window, out of paper and move that window around, over the letters and photographs on the page of a magazine. I asked them to move it around until they found something interesting and then to enlarge it by eye. I wanted them to notice all the elements, all the various new shapes. For example, if they liked a yellowish shape, they were to paint it large with tempera paint. I wanted to get "artsy" work out of the kids. It was fun, but it had nothing to do with them and nothing to do with their childhood.

I taught other things related to adult art, of the sort I myself had done as an artist. I set up still lifes. I taught oil painting to eleven- and twelve-year-olds. (I was able to show them the whole setup, and they found this exciting.) But this was not art across the board for children of all ages. I had not yet found a way to reach most of them.

Although my general approach produced some results with the older children, it just didn't work with the younger ones. I had no clue about what I was asking them to do. I began to feel angry toward the five-year-olds for not painting beautiful designs that could be displayed on the classroom walls. I started giving them irritable looks. Yet I knew all this was off the mark. I said to myself, "Something is wrong here. Something is very wrong."

Although no one at the school had ever expressed any dissatisfaction with my work, I was experiencing long-term panic. The only thing I had going for me was that I was crazy about kids. As I began to teach art, my tremendous affection for them made it possible for me to get through some bad years. But whatever trivial things I did, at least the children in my classes seemed contented enough.

Still, I knew I had to be much better in order to be good. I had to start learning how to teach art to *children*. So I scrambled. I studied. I took courses. I read every book I could find on the subject. It took several years, but I finally broke through. The turning point came when I signed up for a weekend seminar at Bank Street College with Lois Lord. As a result of her teaching, I always start with a child's life and then take it from there.

I feel my strongest sensibility is my tremendous trust and regard for children, combined with a strong respect for the materials I offer them. Perhaps my earlier failure has been counterbalanced by the success that eventually came. I've now been in the field for twenty-five years. I know what I'm doing. I was never trained to be an art teacher, but I find myself working happily with my children and training others in those skills I learned the hard way.

THE ART

OF TEACHING ART

TO CHILDREN

THE BASIC APPROACH

"Nobody can ever tell you that you are doing something wrong in art." —Josh Correa, age ten

My philosophy of teaching art can be stated simply. I think primarily in terms of art materials. I teach long-term familiarity with these materials so that the children can master them and use them to express their own life experiences. My goal is to have the children feel so comfortable and confident with these materials that they are willing to use them to speak about their innermost thoughts and feelings. I see the materials being as much the teacher as I am.

I work with children from ages five to ten. My art room is on an upper floor of the school building. It features a number of tables and shelves, a drying rack, a sink, and several bulletin boards. I work in a private school setting with about a dozen children at a time. I know this is not like a public school, but certain aspects of my experience are readily transferable to larger groups and to children who do art at home with their parents.

In the art room, I strive to create a working environment, an accepting atmosphere in which the children can feel safe, comfortable, and emotionally secure. I want their art experience to be exploratory, to be unthreatening and fun. Some of the kids are only four years old when they arrive. They have to walk up several flights to reach the art room. It's a whole new space for them. They have to learn to trust it.

I try to set the stage for such trust on the first day. I welcome the children warmly and introduce the room to them. In a sense, I begin by "teaching" the room. I tell them, "Everything in this room belongs to the children in this school." I say, "You can get your glue there." "That's called a sink room, where you can get your water." "Your teacher will come back to get you." The basic idea is to make them feel comfortable about moving about in the space. I want to make sure they are not overwhelmed by their experience, that they will find success and pleasure here. I have observed that, given the opportunity, most children will plunge into art with confidence and joy. I want them to retain that wonderful spontaneity.

My program covers six basic art areas: collage, painting, clay, drawing, printmaking, and construction. For each of these, I order materials that are satisfying to the eye and stimulating to the touch. I start with an open-ended exploration of the materials with all the age groups. I believe that this exploration in the beginning is much more important than seeking any specific results.

Some teachers may feel terribly burdened by thinking about how they want things to look and by trying to march the kids step-by-step toward that end. I try doing just the opposite. I'm more interested in the process itself and in having the child connect with it in a personal way. By the time the children are seven or eight, they are becoming skilled in handling the materials, and this helps them to express themselves powerfully.

For each age group, I touch base with all six art areas. In the beginning of the year, I introduce collage, paint, clay, and pencil drawing. Later, I add printing and construction. Often I will begin with two-dimensional work, such as collage and painting, since the walls of our school building are bare in the fall and this is also an opportunity for the art department to adorn those walls. But some years I work with clay in the beginning. I usually don't do the same thing with every class at the same time. (There are practical reasons for this. If you do clay with every class, there will not be enough room on the shelves for the clay to dry before being fired.)

Note: I'm concerned about protecting the children's clothing while they work. I tell the kids they cannot enter the art room unless they have their sleeves rolled up to the elbows. Although some teachers favor floppy old shirts as a form of protection, I think they get in the way. Instead I prefer the smocks made of plastic with Velcro fasteners. These are easy to put on and take off; the kids can do it themselves.

As a rule, I keep each art material separate, so that it can be clearly understood. I believe that a clarity of presentation frees the children to work creatively. Because the human figure is such an important part of the narrative of life, I give special attention to drawing, painting, and modeling the figure. (I also include a lot of social studies art that relates to the school curriculum.)

I see the children once a week. The school year covers ten months, or forty sessions. Dividing these sessions into the six basic areas for each class means, for example, that each class can do painting six or seven times during the year. I have a general sense of what materials I will offer and in what sequence I will offer them. It depends on my reading of the kids' responses. My antennae go out. When I feel the children have really had it with one material and are ready to move on, I head in a new direction. After four, five, or six weeks of painting or collage, they may be ready for something more three-dimensional. When the kids walk into the art room and see certain materials set out and say, "Oh, no. Not *this* again," it's a clear clue to me that we've got to move on. A certain flexibility in planning is always necessary. I keep a record of which child does what as a way of monitoring his or her growth. I also keep a record of the activities of each class, so that later in the year the children can be directed toward the materials they haven't yet used.

I try to extend each material as long as possible, however, to give the kids a chance to truly explore it in depth. Their investigations may require many weeks, months, and even years. This approach produces a rich, personal art, an expression of something the children have explored deeply and to which they have applied their newly acquired skills.

I encourage and respect each child's way of working and let each one work at his or her own pace. (Children are always comfortable at their own level.) I want to make sure that the things they do in art don't overwhelm them, that the children, with their differing abilities, can find success in whatever they do.

I intervene as little as possible, while setting clearly defined limits as to what use of materials is possible in a given class. I try to keep myself out of the work so that it can come totally from the heart and mind of the child who produces it.

I never feel that something a kid has done is really awful, although I might feel it's slapdash because he hasn't been paying enough attention to his work, but has been yakking to his neighbor about baseball for ten minutes instead. I would intervene then because I'd expect him to be more involved in what he's doing.

If a child is happy with his work, then I'm usually happy with it too. If a kid is discouraged, if his work isn't going very well, I will tell him, "This sometimes happens. You've worked hard on this. Put it over there and try another one." Children don't tend to get off track too often. But they sometimes do, and we can all learn something from our failures.

Observing the Work

How an adult responds to the child's artwork is extremely significant. It's important that a grown-up not project his or her own ideas onto the work. Asking a five- or six-year-old what his painting or drawing represents can be confusing. The painting or drawing may have one image along with many additional shapes and lines, added for the purposes of design. The teacher must strive to understand the child's aims and can accomplish this by paying close attention to what is happening. Many teachers ask the kids to explain what they're doing. I try not to do this because the work itself will tell me loud and clear if I look at it carefully. Active and close observation helps one get in touch with the child.

I rarely ask the kids what they are doing, because this would make them switch to their logical mind and become verbal rather than visual. They may not know exactly what they're doing, so we would both be stopped cold at that point. Maybe they didn't think about what they were doing, so I just try to follow them.

Adult responses succeed best when they're nonjudgmental and are as specific as possible. It is important for the adult to refer to the process in which the child is involved and to make descriptive comments about it. By describing to the child his or her exploration, the adult reinforces the child's own discoveries. The interest the adult shows is contagious. The constructive attention given the children helps them to flourish.

As I look at the work, the kind of comments I would make to the younger children might be:

- Let's look at this. Where did you make the lines? Where did you make the shapes?
- Your pencil moves fast, round and round.
- Your line goes all around the paper. That's called a border.
- This line swings to this edge of the paper and that line swings to that edge.
- You have blue at the top and bottom.
- You put red dots on top of a green shape.
- I see a big square and a little square.
- You have a shape on each side.
- I see you have yellow inside and outside the circle.

I might say to an older child:

- The triangle you used is a good shape to show the dress.
- You have made a tunnel, a tower, et cetera.
- Does your train have tracks to run on?
- Those brush marks show the texture of the animal's fur.

To deepen the discussion, as the children move into narrative art, I may ask them a number of questions about their subject and their experience with it. For example, if a girl tells me, "This is a water slide," I will ask, "Have you ever seen a water slide?" She might reply, "Yes, I went on one this summer." I may then ask, "Is going on the slide scary?" I will add that I myself have never been on one. I might also ask, "Did you go on the slide more than once?" "Was the water cold?" "Was the water deep?" "Did you go alone or with a friend?" Such questions can stimulate the girl to recall the actual experience and help make her conscious in a simple way of what she has done. After she has briefly talked about it and resumed her painting, she may remember making a splash and will include this, or perhaps put the friend in the picture. The discussion has made her aware of synthesizing the experience in her painting.

As I go from child to child, I get into high gear. Most of the time I tell them one or two things that I notice—that I think they are trying to achieve. If I try to figure out what they're actually working on and mention it, they will tell me a lot about what they're doing. If it's figurative, it may be a car or a bridge, a dinosaur or a person. If it's not figurative, it may be interlocking shapes or a swirl of colors, which is fine.

Note: I start by telling the children what they seem to be doing and they sort of tell me. My comments help them to review their work and make whatever adjustments seem necessary without my suggesting that any additions might be needed.

My kids can stay on a single idea for forty-five minutes, because as I go around the room, I express a strong interest in what they are doing. By telling them what I see, I invite them to an understanding of why their work is communicating so forcefully. Such comments make the child aware of the consequences of his or her physical experiments. I do think they feel pleased that they put in this effort. This is my way of telling them that they've done something valuable. I can get quite excited about their work. It's just amazing what they do, and I'm the first one there to tell them that. You might say I'm their best cheerleader.

I'm always struck by the fact that most of the children's work looks so thoughtful. It may simply be a design with shapes—not an animal or a person—but it doesn't feel random at all. In fact, my overwhelming impression is that they have been thinking. So I remark about that. I will say to a child who brings me a collage, "You couldn't have done this without thinking about it because you have these pieces lined up and these pieces fit together, while those pieces touch." Because these works are so thoughtful and done with a great deal of care, it strikes me that they have to be meaningful to the children. They certainly are stunning to look at when they're finished.

A remarkable aesthetic quality is most evident in the art of very young children. In their work, four-, five-, and six-year-olds exhibit an intuitive sense of design, but then they begin to lose it. By age seven, the children can become quite reserved and stiff. That's when the art teacher can step in and help them value the things that constitute good design.

I don't, however, teach design and aesthetics as such. I don't say, "Today, we are going to learn about composition." Yet composition is the one design element I always emphasize. When all the work is concentrated on the bottom two inches of the paper, obviously the child hasn't thought about the whole page. I remind him that there are the top and sides of the paper too, and that these must be considered as well.

If the children are just slapping down the pieces for their collages, they are not doing art. But to the extent that they are conscious of pleasing arrangements, balances, and so on, I try to reinforce that. I'm very alert to what is happening in their work. In collage, for example, I look for who is arranging the elements in a balanced and sensitive way and I talk about that. While discussing agreeable arrangements, I try to keep the children aware of shape and color and line. I look for and talk about the variations and repetitions in their work. I look for and talk about the relationships between such elements as the same/different, together/apart, big/little, and inside/outside.

As for playing an active role here and guiding the work in certain directions, I do this after the fact. Although I may point out a need somewhere, it is up to the children to work it out for themselves. I do not suggest the next step to them.

If a child arranges something in an interesting way, I will explain exactly why I find it interesting and talk about what makes it work. I might say, "I see this is a repetition of that." Or, "I see that this reaches all the way across the top." I might say, "You have arranged large patterned papers with small colored shapes in between." Or, "You have three rectangles at the top and you put an arch on the bottom." Or, "Your collage is completely symmetrical." Or, "None of your pieces touch. That's interesting. Look at the great shapes between them. They are like rivers." I can really get excited about these rivers that are the in-between places in the work.

Developmental Stages

In the development of their art, children move through various stages, going first from early gestural work that involves broad sweeping arm motions to simple designs. They move from a primarily motor activity to designing and then figuration. I look for early designing, then complex designing, and then early figuration. But no matter what their age, I try to give the children every chance to go through these developmental stages on their own.

The big distinction in working with different age groups is between prefigurative and figurative work. (By prefigurative, I mean designing with shapes and lines.) You cannot imagine how quickly they move forward once they "get" figuration. I don't push it; I let the impulse be theirs. And I don't set any standards about figurative and nonfigurative work, because I think that would put too much pressure on the children to come up with something that looks like something. To make them think that figuration is more valuable than designing is a real disservice to their actual development. It's going to happen naturally soon enough.

For the five- and six-year-olds, my teaching starts with giving them access to and then talking about the materials. They play with and explore the materials. With paint, for example, they begin by mixing colors. These children tend to be both prefigurative and figurative. Five-year-olds, for example, will play with shapes. The way these come out on the paper may be just fine with the children, who may or may not want to make an image with them.

When they're five and six, their designs become more complex: intuitively balanced, rich in line, pattern, and color. They are so astonishing, so extraordinarily exciting. In fact, they constitute the children's developing vocabulary for making symbolic images that will represent their world.

At about age six, all kinds of imagery begin to emerge. The children move naturally into becoming figurative artists. Sometimes this happens in retrospect. A kid may see something on the paper and say, "Oh, that's a . . ." They notice that maybe the shape is a whale or a rocket ship or whatever—an image they had not intended. Then they begin to be more intentional about their subject matter. The shapes they work with make them think of things in their own lives.

The children may begin their representational efforts with basic images of people, animals, buildings, and vehicles. A big square has got to be a house. A triangle has got to be the roof, and a rectangle is going to be a window. Suddenly there's a bus or a plane with wings. Although it's much more difficult to achieve these representational images, the children push it and begin to render these images with more or less elaboration.

When the children are about seven, they become logical in a concrete way. We see in their paintings and drawings the earth below and the sky above. They figure out there's a world on a flat line at the bottom of the page (often there's a house on the bottom). The sky is way up there on a blue line and there's not too much in the middle. It's a conventional, static cliché, but that's the way many seven-year-olds paint. They just love it that way. It's their way of saying, "I've grown up and I've mastered this." But without help, many children would get stuck here.

Motivating Questions

To help the kids move on, I begin to ask them questions about their lives. I think of these as motivating questions, designed to focus on the children's significant personal experiences and so involve them in the creation of meaning. I try to ask stimulating questions that reach into their expressive center, into their hearts and minds. I ask about real life situations where the kids will want to apply their newly mastered skills to depict them. For six- and seven-year-olds, some of these motivational questions might be:

- When do you like to climb?
- What do you like to do in water?
- What do you like to do with someone in your family?

I might ask the seven- and eight-year-olds:

- What do you like to do when it's cold out?
- What do you like to do this time of year that you don't do at other times of the year?
- How do you come to school?
- How would you like to come to school if you could come any way you want to?
- What do you like to do when you're wearing sneakers?

Watching children paint in response to these questions, one can clearly observe their strong emotional connection to their work. They may become so involved that they sometimes seem to be reenacting the experience itself.

The classes for five- and six-year-olds may begin with a motivating discussion about either shapes or colors. Some questions here might be:

- What colors will you mix?
- What shapes will you make?

With the child's emerging ability to symbolize, I will ask further questions about people, animals, vehicles, buildings, and places. You can see the children's faces light up as they come up with their answers. It's the beginning of a lively involvement. I try to keep our discussions brief, usually under five minutes, so that most of the class time can be spent hands-on with the materials. When I ask the questions, the children usually respond verbally at first; then they are ready to speak through the materials themselves.

The Real World

Interestingly enough, kids don't care about depicting how things look and work in the real world until they are about eight or nine. At that age, they're beginning to get into descriptive realistic painting and these issues become important to them. That's when I might introduce photographs as reference materials, particularly photographs of animals.

Representational thinking for the sevens, eights, and nines becomes more involved in other ways as well. They are moving away from concern with the self to concern about others.

They are observing more details and struggling with ways to represent them. Themes that support their emerging objectivity include social events, figures in action, fantasy, and humor. (Figuration itself moves from the schematic to the particular.) Schematic people become "my brother" or "my sister." Schematic houses become "my building" or "my grandma's house."

The nine- and ten-year-olds also develop a more critical awareness of their own work. They want to learn various techniques that will improve their descriptive accuracy, such as creating a mood and modeling light and shadow. They want to know how to control color, and how to deal with details. They want to know about dry brush, hard edge/soft edge, composition, use of color (primary, complementary, shade, and tint), and about line (whether it's organic or geometric). They are concerned with the creation of space as it recedes from foreground to mid-ground and into the background.

The empowerment of these older children with materials can be further strengthened by showing them examples of adult art. I don't think of this as art appreciation, but more as a source of inspiration.

Because I see art as a nonverbal experience, I encourage the children to develop their ideas about it in ways other than with words. I want them to express themselves in lines, shapes, and images. While learning to read and write, the kids use letters and words in the classroom and at home. When they're six, writing words is really important. You see letters and words coming into their art. You see "I love Mom" written across a painting or a piece of clay. That's all very well, but I ask them not to use letters and words in their art because it bogs them down. I'll say, "You are writing in school all day and you're also doing it at home. This is one room where we use pictures to express ourselves, where we work with lines and shapes."

There will always be the kids who want to write words on their work. The extent to which I can discourage this impulse is the extent to which they will use the vivid language of art. Asking them to use only images frees them up to think with another part of the brain and releases them to express themselves visually. (A very different part of the brain is used in working with color, shapes, and images.)

It is my belief that good, honest materials have an infinite life and infinite value for children of any age. They don't tire of working with paint, collage, clay, or pencil if these are presented as having great possibilities. You don't have to add any glitz to the materials themselves. You can stay with the simple ones. As the children grow up, they can do all kinds of fresh things with the same old materials. They can take the materials they used when they were five and, although speaking the same language with them, can now express ideas that are much more sophisticated.

A NOTE TO PARENTS

For parents who wish to encourage their children to do art at home, I'd like to offer some general principles as well as some specific suggestions. (The specifics appear at the end of each chapter.)

The general principles include creating a work space for the art activity, responding to the child's work, and saving examples of it. How the physical space is arranged depends, of course, on your living arrangements. In an apartment, you might set up a corner of a room. In a private house, a section of the attic or an enclosed porch permits a greater expansiveness.

In any case, there should be a table. Shelves are helpful too, since you'll want to store the materials. It's also important to establish a certain order or pattern for using the materials and cleaning up afterward.

Parents should be primarily aware that art is not about achieving craftlike results; that the emphasis should be on the creative process. When children are given art materials, they will find a way to put them to use. They will usually put them together in a way that is unique and meaningful to them. Let the children come up with their own direction. If they seem to be stuck (which doesn't happen often), a question about a favorite color or a trip they took can spur them on.

Although praising the work may always seem to be called for, the way in which you respond is the key to helping your child's artistic development. Parents who focus on the work and give it serious thought go much further in supporting their children's efforts than those offering blanket comments like, "Oh, that's pretty," or, "I really like that." Such remarks may in fact discourage the children who weren't thinking about pretty or producing something likable, but were trying to match up the edges of the pieces in their collage.

Instead of quickly declaring, "Oh, that's beautiful," pay attention to what your child is actually doing, then describe one thing you observe. For example, you might say, "I see you used three red patterned papers for your collage." Or, "I see that all the blue papers are different in their shapes."

Always place your emphasis on a positive aspect of the work and avoid being critical, such as stating, "Well, this is not such a good part." That can be defeating to a child who is involved with quite another aspect of the work. Focus on what is actually on the paper, not on your own concept of the work, your own agenda. If you start with what you want to see, your child may never meet your requirements and there can be disappointment all around. Some parents will talk about what their child hasn't really done yet. Stay away from referring to what is not on the paper, what the child didn't do. Avoid comments such as, "Well, you could put something up there in the upper left-hand corner."

Some parents are always wishing their children could come up with art that has a better look to it. They wonder how the kids could get somewhere else in their work. Try not to make demands that the children cannot meet. If you suggest that something may be lacking in the work, your child won't be sure of what you want her to do. She may in fact feel she is letting you down. I believe that if you talk to kids about where they are in their work, they may get there. This happens when they're feeling good about what they're doing. Children who are feeling good are generally ready to move on.

If the children want to talk about their work, that's fine. But don't ask them to explain it. They really are not able to articulate what they've done. They have no clue as to where a drawing comes from. Neither do we. There is no barometer to measure that kind of creativity. It's the natural genius of being a child. Instead of asking such questions, enjoy the unique brilliance of your child's work, the playful images and visual stories. Marvel as I do at the creative center from which these impulses spring. In school I will sometimes ask the children such questions as, "How did you know to do that?" or, "How did you ever think to draw this?" My questions are of course rhetorical. I am in fact commenting on the children's ingenuity. They understand this and are pleased with my response.

The art of children can grow richly when someone is around to notice what is on the paper, to describe some aspect of the work and to save and treasure that work. There are two ways to cherish your child's work. The first is how you look at it and comment on it. The second is preserving the work physically. I highly recommend that parents—even those in small apartments—save some of their children's work. This lets the child know that you are responding to his efforts. It sends him and everyone else a message about the value and importance of his work. In school at the end of the class, if I were to let the kids walk out with their drawings and say nothing, they would get the idea that what they did was of no particular interest. Instead, I say, "I've got to have this. Leave your drawing with me. I need to look at it." (Sometimes I'll say to a child, "I want to make a copy of this for myself before I give it back to you.")

You can easily make copies of some drawings or paintings and send them on to grandparents, other relatives, and close friends. When my daughter was six, she drew an angel with a long dress and funny little feet. I had it xeroxed on the upper right-hand corner of some copy paper and it became my stationery for a year.

You can put the work up for display on the refrigerator, held in place with magnets. Or you might even frame a piece or two. Such endorsements should not be overdone, however. Displaying too much work indiscriminately can make it seem as if nothing has been singled out for importance, that one piece of work is much the same as another.

For saving some of the drawings, paintings, collages, etcetera, a special drawer may be set aside in a chest or a cupboard. I also recommend that you date the work on the back so that you can observe the child's imagery as it moves from a frontal view to a profile, then on to a more advanced rendering of the figure. Of course we cannot save everything, but a child is five years old only once. These drawings will never happen in the same way again. The work you save is a unique record of a human life.

I have sometimes been asked whether the parent should work alongside the child. I don't usually recommend this, although it depends on the spirit in which it is done. Many adults are afraid of art materials, so if they say, "I wish I knew what to do with these," sometimes the child can take the lead. I would hope that if you do participate, this would be in the same spirit of playfulness that most children express, which is to investigate and explore the materials at hand. Direct adult participation can also lead the child to realize that art is an interesting, serious, and engaging activity, no matter how old the participant is.

Although adult participation can be fun from time to time, if the situation feels competitive or controlling in any way, it should be avoided. It certainly is not a good idea if the parent seems to be saying, "You should do it this way. You have to put the roof on the house like this." This kind of approach locks the kids out forever. They will think that there is only one way to do something and it is the way the adult has said it is.

Some parents find that their kids are good at art. They are amazed at their children's ability and frequently ask me, "Shall I send my child to a special art class?" Such classes are available in some towns and cities under the auspices of museums, colleges, community centers, etcetera. (They may offer family art activities on weekends.) There are also children's museums and park department programs that feature summer art classes for children. Some of these are excellent, while others are not. You need to check them out.

Although advanced nine- or ten-year-olds might begin to take classes in drawing from observation, it is known that most children don't begin to see that way until they reach junior high school age. So I usually suggest that parents put off considering classes on drawing or painting from life for their children until then.

COLLAGE

Collage, in its simplest terms, is the pasting of various materials onto a background paper. The children in my classes—working within certain boundaries—choose and then arrange shapes cut from paper, fabrics, textured materials, et cetera, putting them where they like and then gluing them down. As part of the experience, they will make their own decisions about using color, size, shape, rhythm, and balance.

The kids sit two at a large table. If crowded together, they wouldn't have enough room for their glue and their other materials. I say, "You need the elbow room." They understand why the minute they get to work.

Before the children arrive, I set a place for each one with a piece of paper, known as the format, which will serve as the background for the collage. The format also helps the little kids—the five- and six-year-olds—to get ready. As they enter the room, it is clear to them that they are meant to sit in front of the paper. When the class begins, we have to have our little hellos. We greet each other and talk for a few minutes because somebody lost a tooth or somebody's dog died. Then we are ready to start.

At the beginning of the year, I teach the routines for collage and I teach the tools. The tools (scissors, staplers, glue) have to work for the children. I've used such materials long enough to know that if you get them right, you get a whole lot right.

I have prepared a variety of format papers for them in various sizes and hues. For young children, the format papers can be seven by nine inches, which is fairly small, yet seems to fit the kind of things they do. For older children, the format papers can range in size from eleven by thirteen inches to fourteen by twenty inches, as well as being smaller or bigger. (The rectangles can always be changed by cutting them into different sizes.)

Using Glue

Glue is essential, but it is a difficult material to work with because it tends to clog up. The question is how to dispense the glue so the kids are not so frustrated that they can't function. If a five-year-old can't count on his glue working, there's bound to be trouble.

I've developed a system for this that works beautifully. I use Elmer's glue, but not from its own dispenser. I've found that transferring it from a gallon container to a series of baby food jars can keep it manageable. After each use, the lid goes back lightly on each jar. (If it were pressed down heavily, it would stick so tightly, you couldn't get it off again. Instead, the lid is just touched down gently on top.) To keep the glue moist, the jars are then covered with a piece of plastic. Although a jar will eventually become covered with glue, it doesn't matter. The lid will still come off easily. If a jar gets too laden down with glue, you just throw it away.

Note: Baby food jars aren't difficult to come by. Just give the new mothers some notice and they'll bring them in. You'll soon have enough to supply you for several years. (Some people may be concerned that since these jars are made of glass, they might break. But they are pretty sturdy. In all my years of teaching art, I've never had one break.)

Each jar of glue is accompanied by a little brush. Before the children arrive, I remove the lids and put the brushes in the jars. I use the skimpy, cheap, soft little brushes that come with watercolor sets. They're fine for gluing, but not for much else. (The watercolors need better brushes.) Although small, they can carry plenty of glue. Such brushes are also flexible, reliable, and work consistently. They can be used for both delicate and large things.

Note: Regular glue brushes are made with metal handles and heavy bristles. They have little flexibility and so don't work well on small pieces of paper. They also rust.

An important part of the collage routine is the drip paper. I put out small pieces of construction paper near the glue. Every child in the class learns that he or she can go get a jar of glue and a little piece of drip paper. They carry both back to their seats, then they put the drip paper down and set their jars on it. At the end of the class, they throw the drip paper away in the trash can. (Little kids drip glue all the time, but because it drips on the paper, it does no harm.)

When the children are done with their gluing, they take

their brushes out of the glue and put them all in a large jar with some water in it. The brushes are not washed out each time, but are kept in that jar with water until they are used again. They can be kept in the jar all year. (Regular glue brushes have to be washed out each time or they become stiff as sticks.)

To store the jars of glue, I cut down a cardboard box a smidgen higher than the jars themselves and keep them there. (The box can be simply stored on a shelf.) After the children return the jars to the box, I gently put their lids back on and cover the lot with a piece of plastic. That's all there is to it. The next time, we do the reverse. We take the plastic off the jars, lift off the lids, and put the brushes in. It takes all of a minute.

Collage Papers

When the five-year-olds have their format paper, glue, brushes, and drip paper, they are ready to select their collage papers. These are precut and presented to them in boxes. The children look at, study, and choose from among these various papers, then they arrange them and glue them down on their format. They clearly understand the format on which they are working, having a sense of the top, the bottom, and the four sides. Some of their designs are exceptionally rich.

It's not enough to put out standard construction paper. Perhaps that's what people think collage is, but it is a lot more. I've thought carefully about the quality and value of the materials I offer. The children can sense how much I love these materials, how I view them as gems. I want to give the children absolutely beautiful papers; they become excited by their great variety and richness. It keeps them involved and their interest levels high.

Many marvelous papers are available. Some can be bought from art-supply stores; others might be found anywhere. They range from construction paper to brightly colored papers to marble paper, velvet paper, and more. I'm particularly fond of the silvered cardboard lids that come with the lightweight aluminum dishes used for hot take-out foods. (Silver on one side and white on the other, these are good-sized disks.) Cut into triangular shapes, they make splendid swords, among other things. Sometimes I buy a special colored paper that can be peeled off and stuck on. It's just wonderful and the kids love it. When this is available, the word quickly goes around the art room.

You also have to scrounge for various materials. You have to see something and say, "That's too good to throw away; I'm going to cut it up." I'm constantly on the lookout for unusual papers, and I save whatever of interest I come across. For example, my daughter picked up a decorative shopping bag, the sort you might get from an elegant department store or an art museum. The paper had a nice thick quality and the pattern was rather luscious. Cutting up that shopping bag gave me about thirty little panels. I knew they were something my five-year-old girls would drool over. (I avoid pictorial patterned paper, however, with the kind of images that the children might want to cut out.)

Sometimes we make our own papers. Hand-painted paper is luscious; it's much more beautiful than construction paper. Maybe I will hand-paint the papers, maybe the children will. We may combine tempera with wheat paste, brush it on the paper, then run a comb or a fork through the wet paint to achieve a lovely textured effect. Or when there's a child's painting that hasn't been claimed and doesn't have a name on it, I might cut it up and add the pieces to our other collage papers.

The nine- and ten-year-olds will sometimes do a marble paper, which doesn't require any creativity, but they think it's magic and love making it. Marble paper calls for four big plastic tubs of water, five little baby food jars, and several tubes of oil paint colors. The kids combine a little bit of the oil paint in a jar with some turpentine, then stir it around with a stick until it resembles mayonnaise. They flop this blob of oil paint on top of the water in a tub and start swirling it with a stick. Then they touch a fresh piece of paper onto the surface of the water and immediately lift it off. Because the oil paint is sitting on top, it will readily adhere to the paper. (Not much oil paint is left for the next child, but he wants to choose his own colors anyway.)

Each kid ends up with a stack of maybe four pieces of marble paper. Drying it presents a problem because there is a lot of dripping involved. We improvise a drying rack, but there are always more papers than shelves, so we have them all around the floor and around the edge of the room. Making marble paper is a one-shot activity, the kind of thing we do once every few years. (I have the kids put their names on the papers before they dip them because they can get lost pretty fast.)

Children are very sophisticated these days, so sometimes you have to grab them with something sparkly. I introduce materials you can see through, such as shiny cellophane, gels, and even old camera film or transparencies. (I once even cut up some of my old X rays.) The five- and six-year-olds hold these see-through materials up to their eyes. They get so excited, you can't believe it. We use fabrics too, but generally stiff ones such as denim and felt, which have a certain body and are easier to cut because they behave more like paper.

Collage with Textures

There's collage with papers and fabrics, and then there's collage with textures. The textures I offer range from smooth to rough. We have sandpaper and cardboard, corrugated on one side, along with spongy packaging materials. There's also the bark of wood, burlap, leather, velvet, netting, lace, and corduroy, as well as various trimmings, yarn, feathers from a feather duster, and felt. (To keep the idea of textures pure, I sometimes try to offer everything more or less in the same color, and it is usually a neutral color.) Because texture is about surfaces, I give the kids access to its "feeling" aspects. I

Matthew, a five-year-old boy, combined rough burlap and netting, smooth brocade, soft felt, and thick leather for his collage, overlapped with pieces of sheer tulle and cellophane

Six-year-old Sabrina made a country house with herself standing in front of it. For her collage, she used materials that were spongy, smooth, and rough

let them feel the softness or bumpiness of the fabrics and other materials. I give them the license to touch everything. That's one of the reasons they love art.

Note: I don't ask the kids to bring any of the stuff for collage from home, because on the whole they don't remember to do it. But I do tell the parents and they bring in many interesting materials.

There is a lot of advance effort involved in preparing and precutting the materials for collage. But offering the children a variety of wonderful, thought-out materials is what makes the activity work. The paper cutter is my key tool. I use it to cut the various papers into rectangles, triangles, and squares. I try to keep the shapes simple. Some days I make curved shapes by swinging the paper slowly and gently as I pull the blade down along the edge to make a soft rounded turn. Or else I cut the curves with scissors. I might give the children crescent shapes or half-circles. Sometimes I give them full circles, although I find these shapes somewhat too specific. (The kids love the circles a little too much, but I may do them just for fun.) I also give them arches, which are useful when the work is symmetrical.

If I'm cutting up three, four, five, or six pieces of paper at the same time, I make sure to put them all in the same box. This gives the child the option of repeating the shapes in his collage. (He can pull out several rectangles or triangles of the same color and size.) I don't tell the kids that they are in the box. Yet many of them will see this and take advantage of it. When they come across two shapes that are the same, something in these children responds. They love to use repeat shapes. (Of course, rhythm and repetition are what design is all about. The variations are what makes the work come alive.)

In the beginning, I usually let the children take as many precut pieces of paper as they want. I tell them, "You can get any pieces you think you might want to use." They see golden triangles and think, *Well, I can use twenty of these*. But of course they use only three. As a rule, I limit the shapes and colors I make available, restricting the varieties to about eight or ten. The children can then pick up as much of these materials as they wish.

Storage Boxes

At the beginning of the school year, I spend some time hunting around for the sturdy brown corrugated cardboard boxes that arrive carrying school supplies. The boxes come in many

Eight-year-old Elisabeth showed a central figure in her collage, holding a shiny silver triangle to suggest a flashlight beam in the night

sizes, from large to small. I collect and save them as though they are precious objects. I cut them down with a box cutter so their sides are only about four inches high. (This makes the collage materials easily accessible.) I set up between four and six of these boxes so they nest compactly inside each other, making for easier storage. At the end of the period, the boxes can be stacked quickly and stored on a shelf.

Each box holds a different kind and a different quality of paper. In one box, I might have solid-colored papers in various sizes, then patterned papers in another, marble papers in a third, and see-through papers in a fourth. These may be cut as long skinny rectangles, or as big fat four-by-six-inch rectangles, or as smaller squares, or as rectangles from one inch square to about six inches by six inches. Others are three by six inches, and still others are three by four inches. I may put out some triangles as well.

There are countless ways to put these papers out. I may set them out by color. Maybe I'll put the yellows and the oranges in one place and the reds in another. There are also days when I offer printed overall patterns and days when I offer solid colors. I do them on separate days to keep things distinct, which is why I also keep the paper collage materials separate from the texture collage materials. (I have to keep order in what I offer the children so they can find order in the art that they produce.)

I also make available a number of small, gray cardboard trays, about eight by ten inches, with a nice deep edge. When the kids are little and need a big supply of collage materials, they can use these trays to collect whatever they want. (Usually, though, the children just pick up the various materials with their hands.)

Seven-year-old Max, using papers with stripes, showed a person surfing (12" × 16"). He suggested the waves by using paper prepainted with brush and ink

*Selecting the materials
they want, the children
carry them to the table
on small trays*

Cleaning Up

Kids often make a big clutter, both on the tables and on the
floor. At the end of a lesson I give them a five-minute warning
to clean up. They clean up everything completely: the jars,
brushes, and drip papers. I tell them to return the materials
they haven't used to the boxes from which they got them. If
the children were to put all the materials back in one box,
they wouldn't be able to make any sense out of that box the
next time. As a cleanup option, I may assign individual children to put specific materials away, such as having one do the
burlap, another the red paper, a third the yarn, and so on.

I always try to make sure that the boxes and trays don't
contain any scraps or grubby leftovers. When I have a class

coming in immediately after, I have to scurry about to pull out all the scraps and those that show signs of previous handling. These would undermine my purpose of offering the kids an excellent selection of materials. Let's say a kid wants to cut a circle for the sun out of a piece of eight-by-ten-inch paper. He goes into the middle of the paper because he thinks the circle has to be cut from the center. (He doesn't think to cut it out of the corner.) Although the paper itself is eminently reusable, no self-respecting child is going to go near it with a hole cut out of its middle. So I take a pair of shears and cut up that paper further to produce two or three small rectangles, which are fresh and ready for use.

Postponing Scissors

At first, I don't give the five- and six-year-olds scissors for collage, although scissors are usually available to them in their classrooms and at home. I ask the kids, "How can you put large and small shapes together?" (Or, perhaps, plain and patterned papers.) Without scissors, they will arrange such shapes and colors in a way they never would if they were cutting up the papers themselves. It forces them to compose with the materials as they are presented. I see collage as an exercise in composition, which can later be related to the children's paintings. (Great compositions usually come from finding relationships among simple shapes.)

Here's another reason to put off giving the children scissors: The minute you give a seven-year-old scissors, she will cut out the tiniest little thing, like the shape of a dog. And twenty-five minutes into the forty-five-minute period, she hasn't quite finished cutting out her dog. She has nothing on paper and she didn't get her dog right. All these frustrations come into play and the child ends up unhappy, with no finished work.

The kids are quite intrigued that they do not get to use scissors, but are happy enough to work without them for a while. (We may tear the paper, however, to get new shapes.) I push my luck in extending the use of a given material as far as I can. Then, when I sense that the children are getting bored, I put out the same materials plus the scissors. One day the children walk into the art room and there are scissors. What excitement!

Sometimes the little kids just keep cutting because it's so enjoyable. Many of them haven't figured out that there's also the gluing process for the paper. I have five-year-olds with piles of little cut-up pieces. It never occurs to them to glue. Why should they when they're having so much fun?

Another day, I may bring out the staplers. The kids can

Six-year-old Kayla fit together plain and patterned shapes in both large and small sizes for her collage

This six-year-old is cutting leather shapes to staple onto his format

staple their papers onto the format instead of gluing them down. If you think you were well loved when you brought out the scissors, the day the children get a stapler is one of the best days of their lives. They just love stapling.

Lesson Plans

In planning my lessons, I used to wing it. Now I go into school with a clear idea of what I'm going to do. I never leave on Friday without a sense of what I'll be doing the following week. During the week, I "read" what has been going on and know that X will be the perfect activity to follow. I have it all written down. I plan out the time, but not three or four weeks in advance. I want to retain some flexibility.

I don't think I ever meet with the children without refer-ring to the previous week's work. There's always the thread of

(RIGHT) When I asked, "How do animals show affection?" eight-year-old Paige arranged torn paper shapes to show a bird family and its nest built on the branch of a tree (14" × 17")

(BELOW) Sam, age nine, used torn paper shapes to depict two elephants (14" × 17"). He indicated a strong sense of design by his repetition of their trunks and the angle of the tree branch

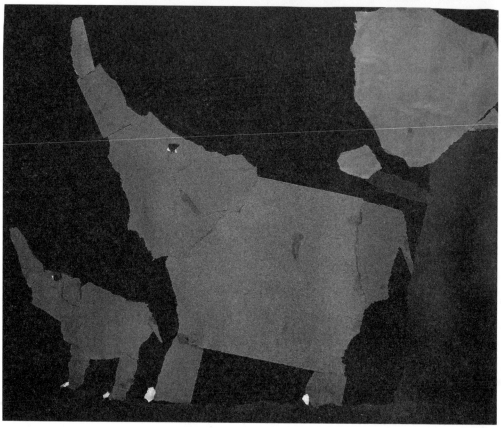

continuity. I might set out patterned papers and say, "Last week, we used solid papers. What do you see today?" So the children begin to sense that there's a logic to what I do, that I have given the matter some thought and that I am doing it for their growth. They know that I'm not being arbitrary, that I'm not just saying, "Well, today we'll do this." I think that's part of the secret of why there is trust in the art room.

Sometimes what the children did one week triggers an idea that leads into the next week's work. I might say, "Do you remember that we had shapes with a straight edge last time? What's this new shape today?" They see the curve. On another day, there might be a softer torn edge. So you've got the straight edge, the curve, and the torn edge. There are several lessons right there, with each one getting its own art day. We talk about that. Every one of these can be magic to a five- or six-year-old, who can get so deeply and richly involved with them.

Or, for example, if I find that a number of children did symmetrical collages the week before, I might teach the class that if a design is arranged equally on both sides, the composition is called symmetrical. Then I will ask them, "Can anyone else make a collage that is symmetrical?" Another time, with the eight- and nine-year-olds, we may use only warm-colored papers for the collage, then follow it with only cool ones, or we may use only one cool color among the warm ones.

When the five- and six-year-olds come into the art room, I might say, "Remember the first days you were here and there was a table where you used to get any of the papers you wanted? Well, today we're going to do just the opposite. I'm going to give you a tray and you can use only the things that are on it. How would you like to arrange them?" They each take a little gray cardboard tray and work with whatever is on it. By being forced to study these materials and to go at it slowly, they begin to find wonderful solutions and to make some amazing things.

The five- and six-year-olds just explore the materials—selecting them, shifting them around, then gluing them down. That's the lesson for them. But for seven- and eight-year-olds, after they have done collage for several weeks and have acquired some mastery of the medium, I will move in and ask them a few questions about their lives. My purpose is to tap into their personal imagery. (I can't ask the children about their lives until they know how to use the materials. That's why I spend so much time familiarizing them with the materials.)

The older the children get, the more I can focus their attention on their own experiences. I might ask, "What do you like to do on the weekend or in the evening?" Or, "What do you like to do with your father?" (Some don't have a father, so I have to be sure to talk about a mother or an uncle or somebody else.) The discussion can get quite interesting and sometimes rather emotional. Then I say, "We've got these materials and we can make a collage out of them. How can you arrange these to show something you do with your father, or your uncle, or your cousin?"

One collage was about a father lying in a hammock reading a newspaper, and the girl comes from behind the screen door and rushes over to him. The girl cut out the figure of the father with scissors, then tore other pieces of paper for the pine trees. She used a piece of cellophane to show the screen door.

One boy, whose father is a lawyer, made a collage showing him at his desk, holding a telephone. It was visually striking, with the telephone wire going down the desk in spirals. The boy wanted to tell me something about his dad, whom he loved and was wonderfully connected with. Because of all that went into the making of that image, I got a whole new reading of this child.

One day, I showed the nine- and ten-year-olds a book that begins with a red triangle (Molly Bang's *Picture This*, Little Brown, 1991). When I asked the kids what it was, they said it was a red triangle on white paper. The book turns out to be the story of Little Red Riding Hood, the idea behind it being a simplification of the forms. Then the wolf comes in. The wolf looks like a wolf, but the little girl remains a red triangle; her grandmother is a larger violet-colored triangle.

Kids of nine and ten are beginning to see how shape can be an analogy or a metaphor for something else. After showing them the book, I asked, "How can you make either a noisy city scene or a peaceful country scene with collage?" They just slide into it like ducks into water. (I taught them earlier about the dynamics of design, and they immediately get the idea that the diagonals and the verticals would read one way, making things active, and the horizontals would read another way, making things quieter.) They pushed some of the elements close. They separated others. Pretty soon, the taxis in a street scene were sparking and making "noise" with strips of yellow paper shooting out from them. The sidewalks were going at an angle and the buildings seemed to be tipping slightly. The children were using many other exciting things they had discovered. It's the kind of buildup that takes time. You cannot get such a sophisticated expression right away. The children first have to have all the days of just being allowed to play with and arrange the shapes they want.

One year, at the end of the term, I was pulling out all the wonderful leftover stuff of collage. I found veiling fabrics and lots of yarn and other textured materials that suggested a portrait to me. I said to the nine- and ten-year-olds, "The room is messy now. There's a lot of texture stuff out there. I want to clean it up. How might you do a portrait with all this stuff. What would suggest a portrait to you? Could this be a veil? What would be the hair?" And they did portraits in collage with some of those things that were hilarious. One was of a woman in a stylish low-cut black velvet dress decorated with rhinestones. She had gold lamé hair. The year's odds and ends had proved to be a rich source of inspiration for the kids.

Pacing the Work

Because each child works at his or her own pace, one will finish earlier than another. The problem all art teachers face is how to keep the class going. While one girl completes her collage in ten minutes, another is painstakingly putting this little rectangle next to that one, lining them all up in precise rows across the width of the paper. By the end of the class, she still hasn't finished. So I will suggest to the first child that she do another collage. I might ask her to choose another size format to work on. I may say, "There's a big table and a little table near the radiator and they have bigger [or smaller] format papers than those you were working on." So the child goes to find a new format and begins to do another one. She might do three, four, or five collages in a period while the other child does only one. I just let the kids work at their own pace and in their own style, so that nobody is ahead of any-body else.

Sometimes the art room gets really quiet. It's the tip-off that the kids are deeply involved. (I'm not just talking about collage.) I haven't asked the children to be quiet. They are simply expressing their involvement in the work by a high level of intensity, combined with a deep focus. They are immersed in the art materials and in themselves.

FOR PARENTS

Parents who'd like their kids to do collage at home have asked:

How do you get started?
You begin by collecting materials for the collage, and just about anything goes. Collage is a whole world unto itself, a medium that can be fun for you to get involved with because you can always be on the lookout for interesting materials. In addition to the materials suggested in this chapter, you can collect paper doilies from restaurants, the wrapping paper from cut flowers, the thick quilted paper from candy boxes, and anything else you can think of.

Is there any limit to the number of materials that should be used in one collage?
The children can be completely independent here and enjoy great freedom in mixing their media together. They can take found objects and put them together in any way they wish. If

they want to include some drawing with their other materials, that's fine. If they want to put paper clips in the middle of the artwork, that's fine too. The children can also use Magic Markers on top of the collage and then glue something over it as well. They can take any materials and make whatever symbols from them that they like. Their choices will probably be meaningful to them in some way.

What supplies are needed for doing collage at home?
You'll need construction paper, scissors, and glue. For the construction paper, I recommend a stack of 9-by-12-inch sheets in mixed colors. The scissors work best when they're of good quality; they may cost more, but they're worth it. (Parents are sometimes concerned about their children using scissors, but I've found that kids can learn to handle them responsibly.)

Do you recommend any particular kind of glue?
Elmer's glue is fine, or perhaps a glue stick. In a pinch, the children can always mix flour and water and make their own glue.

What about storing the collage materials?
You'll need two or three boxes: one to hold the flat construction paper; another for the various fabrics, papers, etcetera; and a third for the trimmings, such as ribbons, lace, buttons, etcetera. The first two might be corrugated cardboard boxes with the sides cut down low, and the third might be a slightly smaller box for the trimmings, such as the kind that stationery comes in. To save space, the boxes should be set up so they can nest inside each other.

DRAWING

Drawing is the most expressive of mediums, providing as it does a direct route outward from a child's heart. Whenever pencil and paper are available, children will automatically draw. There's something so immediate about pencil and paper. Kids spend hours after school drawing at home.

Tools for Drawing

The drawing tools I offer—along with various pencils—include charcoal, chalk, and pen and ink. I also provide Cray-Pas, which are thick, waxy, luscious pastels, a grade above crayons. Sometimes I offer long strands of thin wire as a kind of drawing tool. The wire, linear in itself, is like a fine line. When the children shape it, they are, in effect, drawing in space. Our paper for drawing includes newsprint, better drawing papers—both smooth-surfaced and rough—as well as charcoal paper in various hues.

For the pencils, I favor ebony pencils with their rich, dark

graphite. (They produce a luxuriant velvety black.) I also provide a variety of pencils in differing grades of softness and
hardness, from grades B to 6B, whose line characteristics vary
from thick to thin. I present these on a tray. The children can
choose the ones they want. I tell them to experiment and see
if they like the very dark pencils or the medium ones.

*Note: I sharpen the pencils before the children arrive so that they
needn't sharpen them themselves, which might be disruptive.
What's more, the sound of the sharpener can interfere with their
concentration and mine.*

The charcoal we use is the standard heavy, dark variety,
known as French Ordinary. It makes possible rich drawings
that you could not get with a pencil. Although I love pencils,
charcoal permits a whole other level of drawing, with its gra-
dation of rich darks to soft grays. And if you think you didn't
get your drawing right, you can always rub it off with the side
of your hand. I like to show the children drawings of apples
done by Cezanne. If, for example, he didn't like one side, he
would change it, but leave all his sketch lines in. You can lit-
erally see his thinking. You can see what seem to be mistakes,
but are not mistakes. They're his way of organizing the drawing. I tell the children, "It's perfectly all right to see these cor-
rections. You don't have to feel you've got to get everything
right the first time." (For this reason I discourage the use of
erasers.)

The older children—the eight- and nine-year-olds—work
in pen and India ink as well. (I don't give these to the five-
and six-year-olds.) I explain that the ink is indelible and they
should not spill it. If it gets on their clothing, it cannot be removed. To keep things neat, I set out a sheet of newsprint for

each child on which to place his or her drawing paper. Before the children arrive, I set out a box with the bottles of ink at the side of the room and take the tops off the bottles.

We use crowquill pens, which are made of wood with metal nibs inserted. (People once used them for writing.) I show the children how to hold the pens with the rounded part on top. I explain that the pens don't hold very much ink and that they will have to keep dipping them. I also make brushes and wash available. The brushes are a nice and not too fine sable. The wash is a half-and-half mixture of ink and water, made available in baby food jars. The pens and brushes are in separate boxes. At the side of the room there are also small metal trays, so the children can pick up their bottles of ink, jars of wash, brushes, and pens all at once and go to work.

Note: As with my other art classes, the children get their drawing materials at the beginning of the period and return the unused materials to their original places at the end.

Grades of Paper

For paper, I provide great quantities of newsprint for making large, quick figure drawings in charcoal. For a more extended charcoal study, I use a paper that comes in many shades of gray, green, blue, and cream in addition to white. For pencil drawings, I provide a good-quality paper.

Before the children arrive, I work at the paper cutter, producing a batch of sizes that range from twelve by fifteen inches down to six by nine inches, along with other sheets in between. I divide the papers into two general groups, setting them on resource tables at the side of the room—the bigger pieces on a big table and the smaller ones on a small table. I invite the children to pick the size they think they'd like to work on. Young children like to work large. With them, it's a big, gestural activity. Kids also like to work big and bold when they use white chalk on black paper. Because colored pencils are quite delicate, they tend to work small with these.

Note: Some kids will do several drawings in a given period. Others will do just one. If a child finishes a big drawing early, I might say, "Can you try a little one?" If he or she did a small one, I'd say, "Now can you do a big one?"

When the nine- and ten-year-olds are introduced to pen and ink, we begin by doing a little warm-up exercise. I pass out sheets of paper, about six by nine inches. I ask the children how they might show, in one corner, grasses blowing in the wind, then the fur of an animal in another, and water at the beach in the third. Then I myself might draw a pear or an apple in the fourth corner to demonstrate how cross-hatching can show the form or the modeling of the fruit.

To indicate one way of drawing water, I might show them the Monet painting at Trouville, where the repetition and rhythm of the waves is quite clear. I sometimes will hang a child's drawings up near the Monet painting to demonstrate the similarities. I also show them various Van Gogh drawings in ink.

Drawing As Lines

I want the children to think about drawing as lines, not as filled-in shapes. Drawing, after all, is a linear matter. I therefore see line as a drawing activity and color as a painting activity. I think it's confusing for children to mix the two, although they mix them all the time at home, where they have Magic Markers, crayons, and coloring books. The filling-in they do then is not really drawing, so I don't encourage inking-in the spaces in class.

If a child is going to draw a sailboat in pen and ink, for example, he will draw the sail's triangular shape, then fill it in solid. But once he makes large areas solid, he has left the linear world of drawing and entered the world of painting. I tell the children that even with brushes, they can draw with line and with textural marks. I tell them that they can dip their brushes in wash and still remain in the world of line.

One boy was drawing a boat in the water. The vessel was surrounded by wonderful rhythmic, wavy lines. He then covered these lines with a big, black filled-in area. When I saw the water's lines disappear under the solid black, I said, "This is really a day when we are going to emphasize the importance of line." I discouraged the direction he was taking because he was moving into shapes. He was an older boy and quite bright. He knew a lot about art and about the distinction between shape and line. When I stressed the need to concentrate on line, I think he realized that what he did was not drawing, that it was not line.

Note: I always have the children work on only one side of the paper to emphasize the value of their art. If a kid thinks he has somehow messed up, I tell him to start fresh. Then I put his name on the first drawing and save it.

I might have three drawing activities going on at once. When the kids walk into the room, they may find ebony pencils and heavy paper, other pencils and smooth paper, and chalk and black paper set out for them, each at its own table.

Often I start by saying, "Today, we're going to draw. Would you like to draw on the drawing paper with a pencil, or would you like to draw on black paper with a piece of chalk?" I might add, "Choose anything you want to draw with, but I'd like you to experiment." I tell them, "You can do one drawing. You can do ten drawings. You can do one idea in three different materials. Any way you want to do it is fine." They like the latitude. They go off and begin to explore.

This multiactivity approach opens up options to them and keeps things moving. If there's not room at one table, the children have to move to a table where there is room. It all flows very easily. Over the course of one period, they might try all three of the mediums offered. This exploration helps to loosen them up. There are kids, however, who will sit at one table and work on one drawing the whole time; that is also fine with me.

Sometimes I'll say, "Would you like to draw a person, or an animal, or a design?" I find this is a way of giving them carte blanche to draw anything they want to draw. They come up with their own ideas and just begin drawing. They are often brimming with extraordinary ideas: race cars, lizards, bears, the Titanic going down, pop music groups, and so on. I also get drawings of astonishing sophistication, like a unicorn looking in the mirror and being properly reflected. They also produce rich and complex designs. Every child in the room has an idea of some kind.

Motor Control

The youngest children begin by scribbling with a pencil. (They don't have much motor control.) They start making marks that may seem random, but which are of exploratory significance to them. Then they begin making marks that require a measure of control: strong verticals, sweeping horizontals, spirals and zigzags—all the syntax that is characteristic of the very young. The casual observer might think that it's all scribble, but I find it totally fascinating. As the children evolve, they draw grids, curving lines, and simple connecting shapes. All these elements will later make up larger drawings and images and lead to complex designing, with its own intuitive sense of balance. Then the children will move on to draw people and animals.

When I see a very young child finally make a circle, I could just cry with excitement. Once they make a circle, they usually start adding radial lines to enhance it. This continues for some time. Then their circle becomes a human head, and then a head with two legs attached. There may or may not be arms, but usually there are features: two eyes and a mouth. The walking head becomes a significant event in the life of young children. It's an exciting breakthrough, a milestone in

 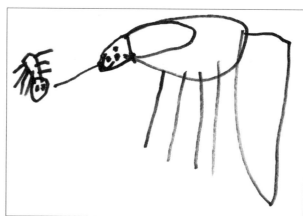

Six-year-old India drew a girl and an anteater (5" × 7")

the growth of a human being. It's the symbol of man, the person. The child's parents are usually excited about the person they see, and of course this reinforces the kid's own enthusiasm about his work.

The child now begins to elaborate on the simple walking human figure. Some heads with legs get their arms right away. When a boy adds a sword to the arm, that represents a masterful achievement. He can get really excited about that. It's not long before he will put a cape and boots on that person. As soon as one figure gets into the picture, an opposing figure may come in. Pretty soon the boy, with his planes and tanks, is into narrative drawing. Suddenly there are battles, with all their explosive lines of conflict.

Often with girls, age five or so, we see the head with elaborated hair, a pretty detailed dress with a triangle for the skirt, and little shoes with heels. Girls also draw families. There's the mother and then there's the baby. It happens rather quickly.

Kristen, age six, drew this princess-bride, complete with crown, veil, and earrings. Her dress is decorated with hearts

The Art of Teaching Art to Children

One boy, working in white chalk on black paper, was doing circles, circles, circles. Then I heard him say, "Home." He did another drawing of circles, circles, circles, and then, "Home." I couldn't figure it out. Then I realized he was drawing a baseball game, with the circles representing the bases. After he did the three bases, his chalk went all around to complete the home run. Suddenly the drawing wasn't just a drawing but a simplified system for describing baseball. The boy had lost himself in playing out an actual game of baseball.

I had one kid who would zip his pencil round and round, zap, zap, zap, like a scribble. So I talked about motion. I said, "Look at how much motion you've got into your line." He would do twenty or thirty of those drawings. No problem; we had plenty of copy paper. I knew he was not going to do this forever, but he apparently was getting it out of his system and perhaps also testing me. But nobody was going to come down on him and say, "No, you can't do this." He was waiting for that. I thought, "When he is ready, he will move on."

While this was happening, the boy would watch the other children draw and listen to me talk about their drawings. The other boys around him were starting to show control, beginning to draw mazes and complicated designs. Then he himself started to do more slowed-down designing. He was doing grids with a lot of horizontal lines crossing a lot of vertical ones.

One of his friends was doing a character from *Star Wars*. Although the boy himself was not nearly that far along, this really inspired him. He began to draw complex and provocative stuff, like people with swords. He did many sword drawings.

Jacob, age six, drew this Coney Island scene, paying particular attention to the fish in the ocean

Keeping Track

I like to keep track of the children's development in art. I give four-, five-, and six-year-olds typing paper—smooth, slick, standard, regular copy paper—and a good heavy ebony drawing pencil and ask them, "What would you like to draw?" I then make a file folder for each child and date all of their drawings. After six months of saving them, I can see a scribble turn into a sword fight or into a mother and child.

The kids want to take those drawings home, but I say, "I'm your art teacher. I have to see your drawings. In fact, I love to study your drawings and sometimes make copies of them, so if you don't mind, I'd like them to stay here for a while." The kids usually go along with that. It makes them feel important. (In the meantime, they are doing other things in art that they can take home.) After six months I give the children their folders to bring home to their families.

Sophie, age seven, drew her pet, "Bik," who chews on a bone, while trying to steal food from the kitchen counter

Specific Experiences

When the kids are seven, eight, or nine years old, I'll ask them about their specific experiences. For instance:

- Have you ever gone somewhere in a bus or on a boat?
- What sport or game do you like to play with your friends?
- What kind of work would you like to do when you grow up?

With the nine- and ten-year-olds, we did a "Summer Notebook" that involved the use of pen and ink and brush and wash. The questions I then asked were: "How would you draw your experience with water over the summer? An animal you saw? A place you went to? A building you were in? A difficult time you had?"

This produced a number of wonderful swimming scenes. Many of the kids were learning how to dive. One girl drew herself on the diving board at the corner of a swimming pool. Although it was difficult to show the perspective, she had the watery lines and tremendous textural lines all over the place. Another girl did her cabin at summer camp, which was beneath a group of trees. She loved using the brush and ink to get the effect of those trees sheltering the building. Still another child did a cabin with all the steps going up to the porch, showing all the proper angles for perspective. I also got the most amazing drawing of a boy on a motorcycle, which was of course a fantasy for that age group; all the lines denoting great power and action were there.

We also have drawing pencils that come in many soft, delicious colors. With these the children work on a smaller scale. I give them little white cards, about the size of a postcard, around which I have quickly penciled in a border to define the space and create a white margin. I do this by using a square of cardboard cut smaller than the card itself.

First, I show the children a real picture postcard with a white border and indicate where their drawing will go. On the other side, there's a place for the name and address and for the message. (Incidentally, they can address them and write the messages at a later time, outside the art room.)

I ask them to make a tiny little picture of themselves for the postcard, indicating where they will be in the summer. I say, "Where will you go? Where would you like to go if you could go anywhere you wanted? You might go to another city. You might go to camp or to the beach." I've done such cards with children of various ages. We usually do them in the late spring, when they may be thinking about their summer vacations. The children make these tiny little pictures of themselves at the beach or wherever they think they might be. You can get little stripes on a beach umbrella with the little colored pencils. The world of colored pencils is a small universe of its own.

Sometimes I cut down self-sticking white labels to the size of postage stamps. The kids then design stamps to go with their postcards. They pull the "stamp" off its backing and stick it on the card. (With a real stamp on, they can actually mail the card.) One year I wrote a little note on each card and mailed it back to the child who had made it.

Drawing from Observation

I had read Nancy Smith and the Drawing Study Group's *Observation Drawing with Children*, which is about drawing from observation. The book recommended a two-pronged teaching approach that I liked. It suggested that the teacher first start an all-encompassing discussion about whatever the children are going to draw in order to focus their attention and sharpen their perceptions of the objects at hand. Then the children draw the objects themselves.

I have the older kids work from observation. They do both still life drawings and drawings of the human figure. For the still lifes, they draw with pencil and paper; for the figure drawings, they use either charcoal or brush and wash.

For the still lifes, I set up certain objects on a table in the middle of the room. One setup involved a wine bottle, a pitcher, a jar holding philodendrons, some fabric, and a big wooden apple. In our discussion about these, I asked the kids, "Well, what do you see?" They replied, "I see a wine bottle." "I see a pitcher with a lid." They named everything right down to the fabric on the table.

As we talked, I realized that many of the shapes of the objects could be reduced to classic squares and circles. After the children had named everything, I asked, "Well, what are the shapes you are looking at?" One kid said, "This one has absolutely straight sides." Another said, "This one is round except for the top." (Of course, when you're all sitting around a still life, everyone sees it from a different angle.) I said, "If you

Aaron, age nine, drew a still life in pencil with a strong, deliberate contour, based on direct observation (15" × 18")

were up above it, looking down, what would the shape of the top be?" "Round," one girl said. I pointed out that since we were not above it, but rather looking at it from the side, the top had become an oval or an ellipse and the bottom did too. So we described all the shapes we saw in that still life.

I then asked them, "Which of these objects do you think might be one of the hardest things to draw?" I was thinking about the wine bottle. The kids answered, "The philodendron." I said, "Maybe, because it goes every which way. But it's the sort of thing you can work out without too much trouble." Finally the kids came to the wine bottle. They realized that the glass wine bottle presented more of a challenge. Because they could see through it, they would have to do the inside as well as the outside. We also talked about the other still-life objects on the table, noting how close they were to each other, and whether or not they were touching. By the end of our discussion, the children were raring to go.

Where you start a still-life drawing is critical. One child asked, "Can I start with the table?" I said, "You can, but I would not encourage it because you are going to find that the things have to sit on the table and that might be easier to show if you draw the table last." I said, "I think if you start with a simple object in the middle, you will soon find your way around." I wanted to keep the children from getting frustrated. After they had drawn the main objects in front of them, they were able to locate the space for the table. It worked. They drew their still lifes with pleasure and with great success.

When they were finished, I was impressed, but I didn't want to make any comments of my own. I wanted the children to do the talking about the work. So I tacked up their drawings on a bulletin board. Then I had them sit down, look at them, and discuss them. We talked about the drawings that were more gestural and expressionistic, and about those where the children had worked slowly to find a clean, clear way to say everything. What impressed me was how appreciative all the kids were of one another's work.

Sometimes I present the same objects to the same group but have them use different tools to draw them with. If they did a still life in pencil in one session, I'd ask them to do a similar setup with Cray-Pas in the next. The children were excited about doing this. They said, "Can we do this longer?" They begged for more. They asked for a special course, an elective in still-life drawing, but there wasn't room in the school schedule. So I encouraged them to go home and set up a similar still life. I often tell the children to draw on their own, both from life and from memory. They sometimes bring in their drawings to show me what they're doing at home.

Another time we drew a bicycle from direct observation. One of our teachers travels back and forth to school on a bike, and I asked her if she wouldn't mind bringing it to the art room one day. When the kids walked in, there was a full-sized bicycle sitting on the floor. I said, "Why do you think this is here today?"

Unlike other sessions, where we talk for less than five minutes to allow more time for hands-on work, we talked about the bicycle for at least fifteen minutes. We talked about the gear and the wheels and how the gear is connected to the back wheel. We talked about the tires, the pedals, and the seat. We described everything we saw, then we talked about their shapes, which were round, triangular, horizontal, parallel. I asked the children, "How many think you can draw this?" They could not wait to draw what they had just studied so carefully with their eyes. Before they began, I said, "Where do you think you'll start?" One child said, "I think I'll start with the seat." I said, "I think that's a good place." Another said, "I think I'll start with the tires." I said, "That's a good place too." The kids were tremendously successful with their bicycle drawings.

Figure Drawings

The older children always like to do figure drawings, especially when they study the classical cultures of Greece and Rome. Figure drawing calls for a model, and every child is eager to pose. So I write all their names down on slips of paper and put them in a jar or a hat, like in a lottery. Although the art room can sometimes get disruptive and chaotic, it becomes totally still when I pull out a slip and call out the name. I ask that child, "Do you want to pose?" They all say yes. Sometimes I have one or two children stand or sit in the middle of the room. (When there are two models, the drawings are of course more complicated and take more time to do.)

I explain to the children that they can pose only if they are absolutely quiet and ready. I tell them they can choose a pose, such as serving in tennis, throwing a basketball, or hitting a baseball. They take a pose and then freeze in that position. I tell them that modeling is really very difficult. I say, "It's harder than you think. You have to sit or stand for a long time, maybe five minutes. And you must keep your eye on one thing." I tell the kids, "There's no way you can hold the pose for five minutes." They say, "Yes, I can." (They try to hold the

Ten-year-old Robell drew from memory a well-proportioned basketball player with extended arms and a bent knee (6" × 8")

pose and are pretty good at it. After five minutes, I give them a break.)

Note: This is when I achieve tremendous self-control in the art room. I get it by controlling the models. If they are disruptive in any way, I say, "Sorry," and simply take another name out of the hat.

We do our figure drawing mostly with charcoal rather than with pencil. The children love charcoal. They work on big sheets of paper, eighteen by twenty-four inches, positioning the sheets lengthwise—not horizontally—to accommodate a standing figure. In one period they might do seven or eight quick sketches. A lot of the work is done on newsprint, but later on I might give them real charcoal paper. I wait until they've warmed up a little since the charcoal paper is quite expensive.

The kids love figure drawing. I think that sitting in a circle around the model makes them feel quite mature. They are focused and find the experience deeply satisfying. While they're looking at the model and drawing, I go around the room and talk to them about their work. When they get to be eight or nine years old, we can talk about the differences between drawing from life and drawing from memory. The children are just beginning to notice that there's an enormous difference between the two. For example, one would rarely think to draw a three-quarter view of a head or of a figure from memory, but when someone is sitting in that position, that's how it will be drawn.

When they work from memory or imagination, the children are free to put the elements in their drawings together in any way they wish. So I respond to that work in one way. When they are working from life, I critique their drawings in another way, because we can both look at the object being represented. I can be more specific here and express more judgment about what they are doing. I can point out that the arm starts near the ear, or have them observe how far the arm drops down. I can ask them to think about the round contour lines of the clothing at the neck, wrist, and waist by observing how it conforms there to the shape of the figure.

When it comes to figure drawing, some kids have trouble drawing what they see. One girl was in near agony because she found it so difficult to draw what she was seeing. Although I try to talk about the strengths in the children's work whenever I can, there are some who are just not able to draw from observation. I may say to them, "Some of these things are really hard. This is not going to be your strong thing that you find easy to do. It's something you have to practice for a long time. You're still young." The general spirit of the room, however, is good because all the kids are trying to capture the figure in their drawings and most of them are succeeding.

Note: There's a difference between drawing the figure and doing a portrait head. I keep the two separate so that the whole class is drawing either one or the other. If a kid is spending too much time on the face when the lesson is supposed to be figure drawing, I try to help him or her understand the satisfactions of doing the entire figure.

Another technique for familiarizing eight-, nine-, and ten-year-olds with the figure, particularly the figure in action, is a simple system involving strips of paper. I set out these strips on a tray—all cut to the same size, about one-half inch by one and one-half inches. The children need eleven strips to create their figures: three for the trunk and head and eight for the limbs. One strip becomes the head, the next two are for the upper and lower torso, and there are two each for the arms and the legs. The idea is to create an articulated figure whose arms, legs, and torso will all bend. (That's why each limb calls for two pieces instead of one.) Kids never seem to understand that the arms have elbows, the legs have knees, and the arms are joined to the body at the shoulders.

I start by demonstrating a sample figure, such as a basketball player. I show how both his arms can be raised up into the air. (The ball itself is added later.) Then I ask, "How can you

Ruthie, Cecily, and Chaz, all age ten, drew portraits of their fellow students, using bristle brushes and ink. The simplified shapes are based on some Picasso portraits, studied earlier (12″ × 18″)

Using charcoal, Cray-Pas, and the "sausage" drawing technique, Greg, age nine, showed a number of figures in action in a baseball game (11" × 17")

put these strips together to do two figures in action?" Or, "If you really want to challenge yourself, how can you do three figures in action?" So a boy might decide he wants a baseball player sliding into the base and being practically horizontal. Then he has the catcher trying to catch the ball, while the umpire stands by. The children move the strips around until they feel they have captured the action they want, then they glue the strips onto a sheet of regular white drawing paper, eighteen inches by twenty-four inches.

While step one is arranging the strips and gluing them down, step two is painting them. (Most of these action figures end up as finished paintings.) The children can take a piece of charcoal to round out the head and extend the body. They can add the hands, the feet, the shoes. They may put in the catcher's mitt or a number on the basketball player's shirt. Then they paint over the figures with tempera. (The glued-on strips may virtually disappear under the paint.) This technique has proven particularly popular because it's simple to apply, with invariably successful results.

A variant I use to strengthen the children's ability to show figures in action involves direct drawing. Perhaps a few weeks after doing the strip people, I will follow up with the "sausage" people. Here the eleven strips of paper are replaced with eleven ovals, or sausages, drawn in charcoal. The children simply transfer the strip idea to the "sausages." The figures here have one oval each for the head, upper body, and lower body, and two ovals for each of the limbs. What works especially well with these charcoal drawings is the use of Cray-Pas to cover the charcoal lines and build up the forms. The children can now add flesh tones for the head, arms, and legs, show the clothing, and render various other details.

Wire As a Drawing Tool

With the nines and tens, we sometimes use wire as a drawing tool. After they've done drawing from observation for several weeks, I'll hold up a long, thin piece of wire and say, "Here's the same thing we've been working with, except that this time the line will be in space." I ask them, "How would you like to draw with this wire?" We talk about how, by shaping the wire, they can do a face or perhaps a dancing figure or someone sitting in a chair. I show them photographs of Alexander Calder's wire animals and circus subjects. The kids can work in wire for two or three weeks, and if they are doing animals, they may want to make these more dimensional. So we

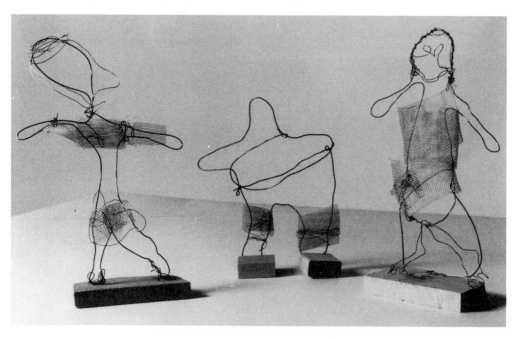

Eight- and nine-year-olds drew figures in space, using florist's wire, with pieces of mesh screening added to create a sense of volume

Five-year-olds used bits of collage materials as the starting point for imaginative drawings such as this turtle and mouse

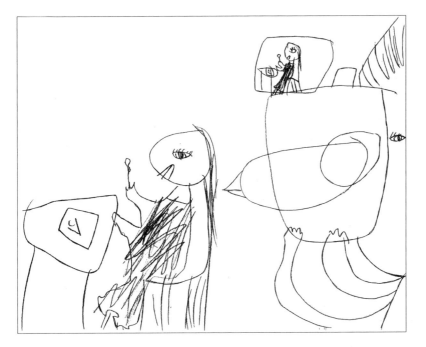

Sophie, age seven, saw herself photographed by the camera at the right while she drew. Her image was repeated in the view finder

may get out some metal screening material and bend it around the wire to enhance the three-dimensional effect.

Before the art class ends, there are always the kids who have finished their work before the others. I usually encourage them to go off and do another collage or whatever they were doing. But there are times when a pencil drawing seems like a perfect activity for the last few minutes. The spontaneous drawings the kids do then are often rich, exciting, strong, and personal. I am convinced yet again that kids have within themselves this tremendous world of ideas. They are not at a loss about what to draw.

FOR PARENTS

Parents who'd like their kids to draw at home have asked:

Might drawing be a good first step in starting the child's art activities?
It's the simplest of all. Drawing is easy for you to handle since it requires only a pencil and paper.

Are any special pencils required?
Although there are special drawing pencils, a plain old number two yellow pencil with an eraser is fine. But if you buy several different kinds and put them in a nice little container, the children will find them inviting. Children also like separate erasers; rubber or gum erasers can do the job here.

Is it important to keep the pencils sharpened?
Absolutely. Children like their pencils sharp. Although the pencils can be sharpened by hand, there is nothing like a good pencil sharpener. If you want to get your child a nice gift, I recommend the electric plug-in sharpeners, which are available almost anywhere.

What about the paper?
For general drawing, the paper can be plain, very smooth copy paper. But you need plenty of it; you cannot be miserly with the paper. There is nothing so freeing to a child as having a big stack of paper available to him. If he has only a small stack, he might not even want to draw. But if there's a good-sized stack sitting in front of him, his ideas can flow freely. (Your child may bring you three drawings before breakfast.)

So if you're going to buy a ream of copy paper for your computer, buy another ream of the same paper for your child. With a sharp pencil and an abundance of paper, the drawing can really get going.

What about setting up things for the child to draw?
There's no need to set up anything special. In my experience, most children are hardly at a loss for ideas. Then, when they get to be nine or ten, they can begin to draw from observation. They might take an object such as a pitcher or a skateboard and try to draw that. Or it can be fun for you to set up a still life for the child to draw. This is something that my mother did with me.

So there are two kinds of drawings: one from imagination and one from observation?
Yes. When I see children at about age eight or nine beginning to draw from life, I encourage them to work from observation. I tell them, "Maybe you could have a drawing book at home where the front part of the book is drawing from your imagination and the back part has some pages where you draw things from life." I might also say, "While your parents are sitting and watching TV, just draw them." Or, "While your cat is sleeping on the floor, draw your cat." Or I might suggest that they draw the things that they see in their bedroom. The children sometimes bring their drawing books to school to show me what they've been doing at home.

What about using something other than a pencil to draw?
Children often like to use Magic Markers and crayons or Cray-Pas. These are all fine for color work, but drawing with a

pencil has been an important art medium for centuries. (After five hundred years, we still go to see the drawings of the great masters.) You might consider keeping a file on your child's drawings, devoted only to the pencil drawings without color.

What about drawing with a pen and ink?
I would not suggest ink for drawing at home, although there may be some exceptions with children who have a special feeling for the medium. Once a bottle of ink overturns, it's virtually impossible to clean it up. Ballpoint pens may be all right, but they are not as responsive as the crowquill pens.

Should one try to have a child reach a certain level of skill in her drawing?
Some parents have asked me why their child can't draw better. As I pointed out earlier, referring to what a child is not able to do can be very defeating. Trying to push a child's capacities further than he or she is ready for can be counterproductive.

What if the child seems blocked or unable to draw?
Always start with where the child is. There are obviously children who are going to make a circle for a head. So you have to start there and encourage the little incremental steps they will take. The child might make a stick figure with lines for the body, legs, and arms. You may ask, "How can you show the pants or a skirt?" But that should be all. Your child will move on when he or she is ready. When a child gets stuck in a cliché and does a drawing of a pretty girl over and over, let her enjoy the repetition. After a while, you might ask a neu-

tral question or two to encourage your child to take her beloved image in another direction.

What if the drawings aren't realistic?

Realistic drawing is not the only way to draw. A drawing should follow the child's inner eye. I have found that children who are very weak in general drawing—especially in drawing people—often have a repertoire of their own. They may depict their own little world in terms of special patterns, dancing lines, grids, lyric abstract shapes, and images. One ten-year-old, who was having trouble in school, did three amazing abstract faces that had nothing to do with realism. He did three in a row and I said, "You should frame all three."

This six-year-old girl sweeps paint across the paper with a big, long-handled brush

PAINTING

One of the great joys of painting is not only the pleasure I know as a painter but also the delight I have in sharing the children's experiences as they learn to paint. For five-year-olds, sweeping a big brush loaded with paint across a sheet of paper is particularly exciting. Then, along with their sensual pleasure, the children begin to acquire a sense of control over their art materials.

The Preparations

Before the class arrives, I set out the tempera paint and the necessary materials. There are only forty-five minutes for a class, so if the children had to set up their own materials, there would not be much time for painting. First, I put out aluminum cookie trays in a row, one for each child, overlapping them slightly to fit the given space. On the right side of each tray, I put five shallow glass coasters, the kind that chairs sit on, to hold the paint. (Since these coasters are now hard to come by, small plastic tackle boxes or their equivalent can serve.) The five colors I set out are the red, yellow, and blue primaries along with white and black. The tempera is kept in quart-size syrup dispensers, which have a spout and a handle with a built-in lever. Using these dispensers, I move quickly among the trays, and in a few minutes I have transferred each color to its coaster.

Note: At the end of the class, I will have the children put away their coasters, stacking them according to color on a special storage tray. I tell the kids to be sure they stack their coasters on the same color. (I soak and clean out any coasters that have become muddy.) At the end of the day, I cover the storage tray with a piece of plastic to keep the paints from drying out. The next time, I will refill the coasters as necessary from the paint dispensers.

Along with the coasters, I put on each tray the brushes the kids will use and a small sponge for cleaning them. To keep things manageable, I give the children only one brush to start with. It's a number 8, made of pig bristle, about five-eighths of an inch wide and not shaped to a point. It's known as a flat. I don't use acrylic brushes; their bristles tend to clump to one side, so the children can't get decent control of the paint with them. (The top-quality pig bristles are much better at springing back into shape.) After the children have explored with the bigger brushes, I make available a smaller, narrower number 5 flat brush, whose bristles are a little less than half an inch across. I also set out some big, long-handled brushes, about one and one-half inches wide, in a coffee can. (These are the kind used to paint window frames; hardware stores carry them.) These brushes are good for big, bold gestural work, and the children can take one if they wish to.

The sponge, which measures about three by five inches in size, goes in the upper left-hand corner of the tray. (Before the children arrive, I have tossed these sponges into a bucket of water, then taken them out and squeezed as much water from them as I can.)

In the sink, also before the children arrive, I have set out cylindrical plastic containers—the tall kind used by restaurants for take-out soups. I fill these with water almost to the top—the more water in the container, the more paint can be removed from the brush. The children will later get one of these containers and put it on their tray.

Cleaning the Brushes

I begin by emphasizing the importance of cleaning the brushes as they work. (If the brushes aren't properly washed out, it would be impossible to keep the colors clean.) Right off, I teach the youngest children the two important things about cleaning their brushes: wash, wash, wash and press, press, press. I show them how to tamp down the brushes at the bottom of the containers of water in order to make them "dance" and get the pigment out, and then how to press the brushes into the sponges, which will absorb most of the excess moisture. The condition of the sponges is important; if they are too wet or too dry, they won't work. A five-year-old trying to press his brush into a dry sponge can become very frustrated, because he doesn't know what's going on. (Part of keeping the environment in the art room safe is helping the kids avoid such an unnecessary frustration.)

Note: We take good care of our brushes. We don't leave them in the water, which would weaken their glue and cause their metal ferrules to come loose.

Getting Them Started

When the five- and six-year-olds arrive in the art room, they see at each place a piece of white drawing paper, eighteen by twenty-four inches in size. (It's called seventy-pound paper.) We always work big in our painting class. I ask the kids to sit in front of the paper. I say, "If I were in this class, this is what I would do." Then I choose one child and use his place to show them how to get their painting materials. First I pick up a tray with the coasters, brush, and sponge. (I ask that they please take the first tray in the row; otherwise, they would want to see which tray has the cleanest colors and that would clog up the line.)

I bring the tray to the table and place it near the hand that the child will use. (The children usually don't know if they're left-handed or right-handed, so I may go around to help them figure this out.) The paper is in front of me and the tray is to the right or left. This is the perfect setup. I see the tray as the stage center of the painting experience, the place on which the primary colors are mixed to create dozens of expressive colors.

After the children get their trays, I ask them to go back and get a water-filled plastic container from the sink. (Kids don't spill as much as people think they do.) They put the container at the top of their tray near the sponge.

With the youngest children, the five-year-olds, I begin with a demonstration before they have picked up any of their materials. I start by dipping a brush into some red paint and moving it around a bit on the paper. That's pretty fascinating for them right there. As I swing my brush, I can see the kids thinking, *This is something I'd like to do.* Then I tell them, "I think I'll use some yellow. Is that a good idea?" The kids sort of recognize that if you have a lot of red paint on your brush and then you want to use yellow, it's not going to work. You have to clean your brush. So I show them how to clean the brush. I show them how to wash, wash, wash and press, press, press their brushes. When the brush is ready for the new color, I paint a little with the yellow.

Next I say, "I'd like to try another color. I think I'm going to paint with green." The kids look and see that the colors set out are red, yellow, and blue, but there isn't any green. After I mix a bit of blue with the yellow on the tray, suddenly there's green. It's like a miracle. I paint a bit with the green, then clean the brush again. The tray itself has now become the palette, the center of the painting activity. Maybe this time I'll go for some pink. I introduce a little red to a blob of white and suddenly the paint is pink. The girls swoon. I paint a bit with the pink. Then, if I want to get really dramatic, I introduce a smidgen of blue into the pink and suddenly I've got lavender, purple, violet, or whatever you'd like to call it. Now that's the color everybody wants; at least the girls do. The children realize that they can get that color too. I paint a little with the purple. By now the kids are sitting at the edge of their seats; they are so eager to begin to paint. I fold up my demonstration paper and set it aside. I ask them if they're ready to start, and of course they are. The children then do more or less what I just did.

With the children who are six and older, we begin with

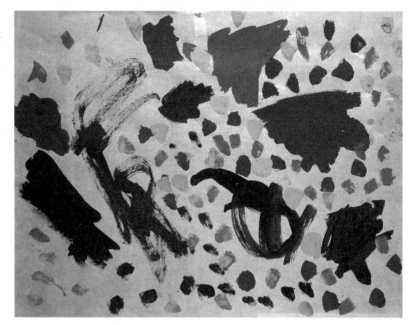

the primary colors, together with white and black; then, later in the year, I may bring out a special magenta, because cadmium red and blue alone can't produce a good purple. I may also bring out turquoise as a raw color. I do this sparingly, because the kids love such colors too much and tend to overuse them. Adding some white paint shows how a color can be turned into a pastel. (I may hold back on the black as a raw color because they tend to draw with it. Yet, if you want to paint a skunk, you need black.)

As soon as the kids begin working, I go into high gear, walking around the room and talking with them about how great and exciting their colors are. I describe what I see them doing with tremendous pleasure. The colors they make astonish me. I also love the gestural work of the five-year-olds, the way they move their brushes around. I tell them, "You can actually see the bristle marks coming across the paper." Some children are real slurpy painters; they just love the wetness, smoothness, and thickness of the paint. Others are more timid or seek a certain precision in their work. Both approaches are fine with me. I will talk about how much this child likes a lot of paint or how that one has painted so carefully.

When little kids paint, their conversation for the first few years is mostly about the colors they can get. As they experiment with mixing colors, the children are playing with this element of art in a relaxed, unthreatening way. It keeps their brushes and their spirits going. It will lead to their expressing something personal in paint.

The kids need two or three years to learn from nothing but the paint itself. The paint is in charge. The paint is teaching them. You can't teach someone to dive into a pool by saying, "Walk to the end of the board and jump in." He has to get on the diving board himself. He has to do his belly flop into the water and keep doing it until his body teaches him. It's the same with mixing colors. You have to do it until you know that you can't get orange by using equal amounts of yellow

This six-year-old boy is mixing colors and exploring shapes and lines. He has painted marks on top of one shape

and red; you have to use more yellow. After the kids have done it the wrong way many times, they will finally get it. It may happen when they're seven, or whenever. After that they'll never lose it. They will be able to do their colors from memory the way any artist does.

Some five-year-olds may cover their whole paper with one color, then paint the next color on top. They just keep painting over and over and over, and pretty soon they have generated a big mass of brown. Some kids may push their brushes into every paint-filled coaster and also end up with muddy colors all over their trays. Now there are no more pure colors and they have no way to make a clean color anymore.

I may try to help by getting them new trays and by reminding them to always clean their brushes. (If any of the paints in their coasters are salvageable, I'll transfer them to the new tray and replace the other colors with fresh paint.) I'm always trying to get the children to respect their palettes, to see how much they can get out of the trays in front of them.

When a little kid begins moving his paint around too indiscriminately, I can see that he's getting out of control. But instead of telling him this, I say, "You really love to move your arm. I can see the motion on the page and I like that." (This is actually true. I love gesture painting.) I might also have examples of contemporary art up on the wall, such as a late abstract expressionist painting by Willem de Kooning, just to let the kids see a nice slurpy work. I'll say to them, "Look how much this painter loved the sweep of paint. You seem to like it too." I want to bring such children back into the realm of painting.

If a kid wants to tap his brush all over the place, and is

smacking it down at random, I might say to him, "You are investigating a mark that this brush makes. If you didn't know that, you wouldn't be able to make these marks at the edge of your painting. This is a good way to find out about things." If other kids begin to copycat him and start tapping their brushes wildly or smacking them down, I'll say, "This child here has been exploring. That is something he is working on." Usually that ends the problem right there. But if these activities are contagious, if they're spreading to other kids who are getting out of line, I will say, "Only *this* child can continue to do this kind of exploring." (The others can do it at another time.)

There are the kids who want to spatter and do nothing else. (This may be an indication that they are out of ideas as well as out of control.) Should they spatter the next person, they will get his or her work spattered and ruined. So I'll say to such kids, "If you get some newspapers and put them on the floor near the sink, you can spatter there." (This will discourage almost all of them.)

I had two ten-year-old girls who wanted to paint with their sponges. Because I knew they were both good painters, I gave them permission. The effect of the sponge combined with their brushwork produced good results and was worth doing. But if their idea had spread to another child, I probably would have refused, saying, "Painting is about what you can do with a brush." I'll ask them to show me what they can do with a brush.

When the children get to be six and seven, they delight in painting rainbows. As I observe this, I always get the sense that the child is telling me she is fully in charge of the colors—that she is able to work with secondary as well as primary colors, and that she has enough control so her colors are not muddy. These ubiquitous rainbows seem to be the child's way of saying, "I figured out all the colors." It's a stage they go through. I'm pleased, but I also know they are ready to move on and do more personal work.

Note: It cannot be too strongly stressed at points like this that motivating questions about the child's personal experiences should be asked to stimulate fresh ideas and original thinking about the work he or she is doing.

On the wall next to the clock, I keep a comparably sized color wheel. It has yellow at the top, then red and blue, with the secondary colors—purple, orange, and green—in between. Beside the three primary colors, I have written the letter *P* in black. The children begin referring to the color wheel a great deal, and they finally remember what the *P*'s stand for. On a day when I'm tired and a child asks, "How do you get brown?" I just tell him to mix the three *P* colors together.

The time comes when a six- or seven-year-old wants to know how to make orange. I tell him, "Find the orange on the color wheel. Then find the two colors next to it and mix them together." Often, when a child asks, "How do you mix orange?" someone in the room already knows the answer and provides it.

When a kid paints the sky a dead blue right out of the paint coaster, I might ask if the sky is ever another color. The child may then think about other possibilities and mix other shades of blue or gray. Or, if a painting includes a street, I may say, "Well, you're walking on the cement. "What color is it?" The child replies, "Gray." I ask, "How can you mix gray?"

(There are many ways to mix gray without using black.) The child will find a way to do it.

As the children get older, they find there are many ways to mix blue, not just the blue the teacher handed them. There's midnight blue, and other great colors they already know. There are countless oranges. There are a hundred ways to mix green. The kids can discover lime green, forest green, moss green. They know they can get army green just by combining black and yellow.

More Formal Lessons

When the children are around eight years old, I begin to teach them skills—the elements of art, the more formal lessons about color, and other painting techniques. At that age, they are opened up and wide-eyed. They love knowing this stuff and they lap it up.

We talk about primary and secondary colors, and about complementary and analogous colors; about how the complementary colors, such as orange and blue, sit across from each other on the color wheel, while the analogous colors, such as green and blue, or purple and blue, sit next to each other. I teach them about how complementary colors bounce off each other optically; how when these colors touch each other with no white paper in between them, they seem to vibrate. I show how analogous colors, on the other hand, do not vibrate optically but produce a harmony between them.

The children might do a painting about a mood, either solemn and gray or lively and bouncy. We talk about how mood is carried by color. They find out how complementary and analogous colors can help convey these ideas. Then, to apply these concepts, I might ask them how they would depict a sunscape or a moonscape, or a noisy place or a quiet place.

Still Lifes and Color

When the children are about eight or nine, I may set up a still life to teach them about color. I might base this still life either on the primary colors or on the secondary colors. Then I will ask the kids to tell me what they see. They'll say: a spoon, a plate, a pitcher. The discussion goes on for ten to fifteen minutes—longer than we usually talk—but I don't let the children paint until they have connected to what they are seeing. Suddenly they realize that the still life before them has been set up for its colors and they know these are all primary or secondary colors. The kids are just knocked out by this concept.

I might show the children the "dry brush" technique by putting out bowls of thick paint (earth-colored here) but no water and many brushes, then showing them how to indicate texture with a dry brush. I might ask, "What would the woolly texture on the back of a sheep look like in paint?" They would then experiment to find ways to indicate this. Playing with paint this way and understanding the movement of brush strokes gets the children involved not only with texture but with showing motion in their paintings.

Although working in color generally means using paint, I use pastels as another color tool. If you give a child a piece of paper and some pastels, he'll use them as drawing tools, like crayons. To forestall this, I will offer the children a handful of broken pastels on a little tray. Their exteriors may look dusty and dirty, but when the children run the pastels on their sides, rather than on their tips, they find they have created some brilliant swatches of violets and yellows on their paper. They go on to develop rich, beautiful designs with these. Pastels have a wonderful way of overlapping, of building up. The children find they can layer them to get a certain mood. They learn they can then work out the layers and smudge them with their fingers to produce the effect they want. Pastels on paper can create a sunset sky or an evocative landscape. I find that using them on their sides is a much better approach than just using them to draw lines.

Note: We don't provide Magic Markers. Their colors are bright enough, but don't have a rich quality. Although Magic Markers can be used to draw lines, the only way to get a decent mass of color with them is by filling in the outlines.

I discourage the children from drawing in paint; I teach drawing and painting separately, explaining that the former uses line and the latter uses mass or solid shapes. There are always a few kids who want to draw with their paint. I am there, however, to help them paint when they paint. So when I see eight- and nine-year-olds drawing with paint, I might do a demonstration to show them that painting is not about drawing. I'll say, "Let's suppose there's a shelf . . ." And I'll make a horizontal blue line with paint about two-thirds down the paper. Then I'll say, "Suppose there's a blue plate resting on this shelf." I point out that one way to show this is by drawing a line around the edge of the plate. Another way is to draw a circle and fill it in with blue. A third way is to take the blue paint and, instead of drawing a circle around the edge, applying the paint directly until the full circle of the plate appears on the paper. This third way, I tell them, approaches the work as a painting. I explain that if they work this way in planes of color, they are going to be in the realm of painting, as opposed to the world of drawing.

So if, for example, a boy is doing a hockey player by drawing around the edge of the figure with black paint, and then using blue to paint in the big leg protectors, I might tell him, "You don't have to draw around the edge. You can make the whole leg by just painting in that whole blue shape at one go."

Drawing before Painting

For complicated paintings, some kids will predraw the entire work in charcoal, and then fill in the drawing as they would in a coloring book. When I saw some of my best painters begin to do that, I said to myself, "I have to do better by these kids. I have to tell them they don't need to predraw so much. I have to tell them that they're so good already, they can just go ahead and paint without these extensive preliminaries."

I had one girl who began a painting by first making a great charcoal drawing that showed ten people at a birthday party, with someone going upstairs and someone else coming downstairs. Some were opening presents over here, and the music was playing and kids were dancing over there. All this was happening on the paper, but it existed only in charcoal. I thought to myself: *How could the girl ever get back into that scene with paint and bring it to life?* She might be too scared that she would lose it. I wanted her to be successful. I didn't want her to be so overwhelmed by her brilliance and skill in drawing that it undermined her great ability to paint. But she never did finish that painting. If she hadn't gone so deeply into it with the charcoal as a drawing first, but had plunged in directly with the paint, she would have painted like a champ, the way she did when she was younger. But here, the great drawing skills she had acquired got in her way.

Sometimes the six- and seven-year-olds, who have been painting for a year or so, need a little jump-start so that they don't have to confront the blank, white paper. One idea I use as a starter is the first letters of their names. When the kids arrive in the art room, I have these letters already cut out of construction paper. The children are pleased to see their own initials set out for them. Ellen, for example, comes up, finds an *E* glued onto the paper, and just grins from ear to ear. Then she marches over to her seat and proceeds to make a design incorporating that letter.

The children may ask, "Can I paint over the letter?" I say, "Of course, you can. You can also set it upside down or turn it any which way you like." Some children create a playful partylike look, with dancing colors all around. Others paint their colors in as if the letter weren't there at all. In any case, it's a way to get them started on a painting, a way to keep their arms moving.

To stimulate the children, to help them continue to explore and gain mastery in painting, I set up a wide range of other formal problems. For example, I might ask the six- and seven-year-olds:

- How can you mix at least a dozen colors and paint a design with them?
- How can you paint a design with the largest and the smallest brushes?
- How many shades of green can you paint?
- How many shades of pink?

- How can you paint with only bright colors? (These are achieved by mixing two primaries, with variations in the amounts.)
- Can you paint a very large and a very small painting in one class period? (Early finishers can do a medium-sized painting as well.)

I also vary things a bit by giving them a piece of colored paper one day or a piece of paper with a different shape and then asking:

- How can you paint on a colored format?
- How can you paint on a round format?

In their paintings, the children are often confronted with the problems of indicating perspective. I try to help when they run into trouble. In one situation, some eight- and nine-year-olds did a large background painting, six feet tall and twelve feet wide, for a school play. It showed a road going back and a fence going off in a series of radial lines. The children just couldn't get the verticals to stay vertical. It was disturbing to some eyes to see the fence posts set at 45-degree angles to the road. We talked a lot about how to show perspective. They agreed to make the fence posts upright and parallel with the sides of the paper and were greatly relieved to see how much more realistic they looked.

Note: Interiors are harder to depict than landscapes, because the arrangement of rooms, walls, ceilings, and doors requires an understanding of perspective. It's difficult for the children to do these, since they have no point of view about where they themselves might be standing in the room, but they find their own wonderful ways to organize these baffling spaces.

Before the children begin a painting, I might ask them, "What colors do you want to start with? Where do you want to start on the paper?" I might caution them that if they start too close to the bottom, there might not be enough space to show all the action. I suggest that they might want to move their subject up a bit, more toward the middle of the paper.

We did an outdoor school mural on the side of the building, and the five-year-olds who participated would not put

When I asked, "How can you paint a person and an animal?" Gaby, age six, showed a girl with her dog (18″ × 24″). I said, "The triangle makes a good shape for the dress. The dog's tail is wagging. They must love each other"

When I asked, "How can you paint a vehicle?" Chris, age six, painted the Queen Mary, *which he visited with his aunt (18″ × 24″). I said, "Your smokestacks push into the blue sky and you have repeated the blue in the portholes and the water"*

their houses anyplace but at the bottom of the mural. In their view, closest to the ground was where the bottom of everything was. They didn't see it as being otherwise. I have also found that six- and seven-year-olds have the need to do this in their paintings. There is nothing you can do to thwart this; it's a developmental matter.

Many children will depict the action of riding their bikes in the three inches at the bottom of the paper, with perhaps a green line beside their bikes. If it's a sunny day, they'll have a few small clouds. Since the clouds are white and the paper is white, they'll make the clouds blue. So there you have your standard cliché painting. Even at age nine and ten, it's hard for some children to get their subject off the absolute dead bottom of the paper. They still don't believe it can be anywhere else.

I'm thinking to myself, *For this painting to be strong, there has to be something going on in the middle*, but often I won't intervene. I just let the painting remain that way. When I begin to feel that a kid can move past this, I'll ask him what he sees around him. If, for example, he's riding a bicycle at the bottom of his painting, I might ask him what he saw while he was out bicycling. I'll say, "Were you in the park? Were you out in the country? What was going on around you?" And he'll begin to remember some fragments. With the eight- and nine-year-olds, I might show them reproductions of paintings where the horizon line is set higher, so that they begin to see that the plane on which things are resting is not at the dead bottom of a painting.

When I asked, "What do you like to do at a table?" seven-year-old Valentina showed herself with three friends (18" × 24"). I said, "You have a figure on each side. I see one from behind. It's hard to do sitting figures but you fit them nicely on the chairs"

With seven- and eight-year-olds, the best way to move them past the clichés, characteristic of their age group, is to ask them motivating or stimulating questions related to their own lives. I might ask them about their families, or recent events, or the weather of the moment (if it's raining or snowing), or about the new play equipment in the schoolyard. I try to ask questions that are important to them so they'll want to answer them in their paintings. The children's responses to such relevant questions can be rich, personal, and even touching.

For seven- and eight-year-olds, I might ask:

When asked, "Where do you like to go when you leave your house?" Sarah, age seven, painted a visit to a restaurant (18" × 24"). I said, "You have painted so many details: the tiles on the floor, the people sitting, and the waitress. You must really like to be in this restaurant"

When I asked, "Where do you like to go in the school when you're not in the classroom?" nine-year-old Gabbi, who likes the school library, painted the bookshelves and many colored books there in the background. She allowed plenty of space to show the table, the stool, and herself (18" × 24")

- What are the times when you are excited or sad?
- Where do you like to go when you leave your house?
- How can you paint people when they're at work?
- How can you paint a place that's special to you?

For nine- and ten-year-olds, I might ask:

- What are the times when you help others?
- What are the times that you celebrate?

Instead of narrowing the situation, asking motivating questions opens things up. If you were just to tell children who are eight, nine, or ten to do anything they like with the paint, it would be like putting them on a bridge without

When I asked, "Where do you like to go in the school when you're not in the classroom?" ten-year-old Erica painted herself in the gym (18" × 24"). I said, "You like basketball. You have painted the gym floor to make a square shape. You are standing inside a circle. I love your reach"

railings—a situation that's too wide open. (In order to feel safe, the children might turn to cliché images like the hearts or rainbows they have already mastered.) But motivating questions focus their attention and invite openness, while not limiting their form of expression. Kids are spunky and spontaneous, and they can invariably find many personal, exciting, and expressive ways to respond.

Children like to be physically active. They like stretching. They stretch when they climb, catch a ball, or ride a bike. If you talk with them about stretching, they will respond. A motivating question might be, "When is a time you stretch your body?" Or, "How can you show a situation where you're stretching your body or climbing?" We then list their ideas on a large sheet of paper that is already up on the bulletin board. These are some of their responses:

- I stretch when I climb on a jungle gym at school.
- I stretch when I climb a tree.
- I stretch when I shoot for a basket.

I've learned to ask motivating questions that catch the children when their memories of certain events are particularly strong, such as when they return from their summer or winter vacations, or from class trips. I will ask, "How can you paint about a summer experience you had?" From the time they are six right through all age groups, the questions might be, "Did you go swimming in the summer? Where do you go? Do you go to the beach? Do you swim in the city's swimming pools?" and so on. By the time we've had a little five-minute discussion on the subject, every kid has become deeply con-

When I asked, "How can you show times when you stretch?" Victoria, age ten, painted herself as a dancer (18" × 24"). I said, "Your body reaches all four sides of the paper. The figure has a sensitive shape, head, and features. You must be a wonderful dancer"

nected with a swimming experience that he or she has had. We might then talk about painting water in various ways.

One memorable painting was by a girl who didn't leave the city. Her father had taken her with him when he went to have the car washed. So this was a painting about their car in a car wash under the rubber strips you drive through. It was one of the most hilarious paintings I've ever seen. At first it looked like a rainstorm. Then it became clear that the black strips were separating around the car. It was such a strong, glorious, vivid memory of what the girl did on her vacation.

It doesn't matter what imagery the children come up with, as long as it is meaningful to them. When I feel that a child hasn't given the painting enough of herself, that's when I really, really work with her. If I feel the work is just at one level, I try to get the child to deepen it visually or emotionally.

When the painting is not meaningful, I feel it's extremely important to come forward and work with the child. To deepen her experience, I will ask questions until she remembers more about it. Because I don't want the children to leave their work weak, I'll ask a series of questions about where they were and what they did. I might say, "Okay, you got around the river and you crossed it. What did you see on the other side?" Or, "You're on a school bus. What's around you as you come to school? You know there's more than just the bus itself." They know a lot about the city, and they can paint about it, so I don't let them get lazy.

I'm always concerned about imposing myself too much on the children's work. Although I try to intervene as little as possible, I'm there to teach art. There are certain visual elements that make art "read," or come across strongly. The kids can learn about these elements from me. I pay careful attention to what is going on and will intervene if I think they're onto something. My role is also to get the children to think about the rectangle of paper as a painting with a top and bottom and four sides, and to see that any sections that remain white are a part of the painting too. I can be very critical about their work in a nonjudgmental sense. And I can intervene in many, many ways if I think they are ready for it.

For example, I remember a painting by a ten-year-old girl of a wedding ceremony, with the bride and groom walking to the altar. The bride was wearing a white dress; the groom was wearing a black suit. You might think they would be standing on a red carpet, but they weren't. The girl painted the white dress carefully, but it didn't show up against the white paper. So I walked up to her and said, "What a beautiful bridal dress. I can see it from here, but I can't see it at a distance." I asked her if she could find a way to solve that problem. So around the edge of the bride and groom she painted the background black. That didn't work either, because then you couldn't see the groom. If she didn't resolve the background differently, no one was going to see both the bride and the groom. So we went back. She was bright and willing to work on the problem. She understood it and was prepared to solve it. She waited until the black was dry and then painted the carpet violet. Because it was an in between value, the violet worked and set off both figures. So the girl's painting ended up being very effective after all.

Kids often have a favorite subject or interest and they try to get that into their work. One girl always included her dog, Nick, in her paintings, but not because I asked the children about their pets. Regardless of my question, she would always put her dog in the painting. Because my motivating questions are broad, such as, "How could you show yourself in a group of people, doing something with a crowd?" she thought about her dog and was able to find ways to include him. When I asked, "When do you see a crowd?" she said she would see people when she walked her dog, so that's what her painting was about. Even on the subject of water, she'd be swimming but Nick would be nearby at the side of the pool.

I had a boy for whom hockey was an obsession. He would put a hockey stick in his painting, show the stick smacking a puck, and think that that was enough. I couldn't let him stop at that; I knew he could do more. He could show where the hockey stick was and include the person who was holding it. I asked him, "Where's the player? Is he at the net, defending the goal? Or is he skating down the ice with it?" The boy had to tell me more about his subject. I also asked, "Where are this hockey stick and puck meeting?" The answer was, "They're on the ice." So then I asked, "What color is the ice?" "White," was the reply. So I said, "Okay, get some white on your brush and paint the ice," because white paint on white paper is much richer than just leaving the raw paper white.

I had another boy who painted about hockey every chance he got. Whatever the motivating question was, he just did a hockey game. When the question was, "How would you show a crowd?" he had the action on ice, but with nobody watching. I said, "Isn't this Madison Square Garden? Isn't anyone watching the game? You know there's a crowd out there." He said, "I can't do it. I can't do it." I keep some visual aids on hand and have photographs that show crowds. So then the boy had to find a way to do the upper seats. He had to think about how he might want to work the upper passage of the painting. I encouraged him to move from the memory of a hockey game to the fact that this was a painting he was doing. It was a big transition for him to make in how he thought about his work.

The children don't need too many reference materials. They have a way of knowing how to do almost everything themselves. Even when a photograph is in front of them, they are essentially asking about how to get that image onto their paper, so I help them do what they already know how to do. If they are painting animals, I will say, "Well, what is the shape of the body? Is it a circle, or a long shape?" They may reply that it is a long shape, and they are able to put that down. Then I might ask, "Is the head larger or smaller than the body?" They may say, "Smaller." Then I will say, "Where is it attached?" They will know where. A kid once got that far with doing an animal, but then asked his teacher, "Where do the legs go?" She replied, "Where they belong." This was all that the boy needed to know.

Note: We have lots of photographs, and the children are encouraged to look at but not to copy them. They have their own ways of understanding the shapes. We do keep a good file on horses because some kids don't know about the angle of the legs, particularly the hind legs. I also keep a file on domestic animals and make several books available to the children on farm animals and on other animals.

Displaying the Work
Sometimes when I show the artwork in the hallways I'll use captions to underscore the tremendously personal way in which the kids respond to the questions. Although I like a

When I asked, "What did you do with your friends this summer?" nine-year-old Rebecca painted herself, her brother, and her cousin on a trampoline (18" × 24"). I said, "You make the trampoline a nice big shape. The figures show up well against the black background"

piece of art to say everything without words, we will use the captions to capture the "personalness" of the children's work. So sometimes I print or type up a simple sentence or two indicating what the children have told me about their work and I put these underneath their paintings. One year a boy did an eighteen-by-twenty-four-inch painting of a big daddy longlegs he had seen on the wall of his cabin at camp. The caption quoted him as saying, "I know why it's called a longlegs, but I don't know why it's called daddy." Another kid might say, "I learned to dive this summer and dove off a high diving board." With the nonfigurative paintings, I may write a caption myself, such as, "Suzy loves to move paint by swinging her arm." These captions are a good way of communicating with the other teachers, the parents, and visitors to the school.

Note: The children like to take their paintings home, but at eighteen by twenty-four inches, they become unwieldy. Rolling them up might seem to be a solution, but the paper invariably curls up and is difficult to straighten out when unrolled. Instead, I gently fold the paintings in half with a slight crease and put them in plastic bags. The crease is negligible when the paper is straightened out. For easy identification, I pencil in the name of each child on the back of the painting where it will stick out of the bag. (The bag itself can hold other projects to take home at the same time.)

Sometimes I will suggest special subjects to the children. I've asked them to paint about love, but you don't ask that unless you have a very close relationship with the kids. One girl did a painting of herself going out on a branch of a tree to rescue her cat. That was her love. But I don't always ask the kids to paint about subjects that are personal and serious. If I did, they would say, "Ugh! Heavy-duty art. I can't take it!" I combine these subjects with design problems such as playing with color, shape, or line, so the kids are not always being asked to delve into their own hearts. I want to encourage exploration in their paintings without their being too taxed emotionally.

Pacing is everything, which is why I try to remain as sensitive to the kids as I can. I expect a lot of them, but I also need to pull back and offer them a place to relax. There are such occasions during the year. For example, on Valentine's Day, we can work with archetypal heart shapes, which the kids have been doing since they were very young. Red and magenta are always favorite colors for them, so we use them in paintings or in making Valentine cards with collage. I tell the kids, "You can decide how many hearts you want and incorporate them in a design." So they play with this.

There are days when I put reproductions of museum paintings up on the bulletin board, with hard-edged examples on one side and soft-edged examples on the other. I'll ask the nine- and ten-year-olds what they see. They'll report that they see abstract shapes and this and that. I keep them looking at the paintings by saying, "What else do you see?" One kid will say, "Well, it's kind of a mishmashy scribbling." I'll say, "Yes, those on that side are brushy and soft-edged, but the others are very tight, precise, and hard-edged." I ask them, "Which style will you choose today: the hard-edge or the soft-edge?" Because these are abstract paintings, the children have a chance to play with the paint. But although they're relaxed, they're nevertheless very involved. After spending the day with reading, writing, and math, they are free to swirl the paint around if they wish. There are no great emotional demands here. They do designs that gratify them. Some kids make careful geometric shapes—rectangles, triangles, or whatever—that have a neatness about them. I watch them work. I can see that it's necessary for them to have this kind of experience. The process seems to be emotionally integrating. The children seem so content and at peace.

Although my approach is essentially gender-neutral when it comes to subject matter and imagery, I find that boys and girls may respond differently, depending on their ages. Boys are often into sports, monsters, villains, scary things, and plane crashes. The six-year-olds will paint Captain Hook, sometimes for the tenth time. They've got some of these characters down like you cannot believe. For them, one more piece of paper is one more opportunity to paint these incredible pictures. I don't discourage this, but neither do I want the boys to feel that they are stuck there, that they can't move beyond this subject matter. So if a boy is painting a rocket ship, I might bring out a big fat brush and say something like, "Well, if this takes place in outer space, how can you show that?"

Girls are often into painting pretty girls. They will do pretty girls over and over until they get them right. To try to move them forward, I might say, "She's a princess. But where is the prince?" So then the girl does the prince. Or I might say, "She's very beautiful. Maybe she needs to be with a friend." So I find ways to get them to move in other directions. When the girls draw or paint themselves, they often do their families as well. They like to do their parents and their brothers and sisters.

Jonathan, age ten, used paper strips to show baseball players in action, then painted in the diamond, the bases, and other details (18" × 24"). I said, "Your pitcher looks like he's just about to pitch from the mound"

After a discussion about immigration and the search for employment, Maya, age nine, painted her father at work (18″ × 24″). I said, "You are proud of your father, who is a sanitation worker. You really know the shape of that truck. You have shown the streets in the city and the buildings"

Note: While the children are developing in their imagery, they need to go back and play too. They move in both directions. One time, they will laboriously and carefully paint various subjects. The next time, they may turn around and paint a mishmash design.

The materials the children use in painting are so basic: the three primary colors, white, and black, along with a piece of white paper. They can paint anything in the world with these. Because I don't know what their individual life experiences have been, I always find their paintings a big surprise. Since children are interested in what is going on in their world, the paintings they make are going to be about their experiences, their fantasy life, and their sense of humor, not mine. So whatever emerges is what the kids come up with during the forty-five minutes they spend in class. They are rarely at a loss

After the discussion about jobs, nine-year-old Ethan, who recognized that teaching is work, painted his art teacher (18" × 24"). I said, "Yes, teaching is a job. You painted me in front of the file cabinet and the arched window. It was a good idea to turn the paper tall to include the whole figure"

for imagery, though it may not be what the teacher had in mind at the start of the lesson. Whatever they do, I'll say, "Fine. Great." I trust the kids. If you offer them good materials to work with, they will grow and flourish. It's natural for them. By the time they're ten, the things the children paint just take your breath away: a dead deer they found while ice skating, the tables and tiled floor of their favorite restaurant, or seeing themselves in sleeping bags at a sleep-over party. There is nothing they cannot paint about.

FOR PARENTS

Parents who'd like their kids to paint at home have asked:

What kind of paint would you recommend?
Painting is probably the most difficult art activity to do at home. At school, we use tempera, which is a wonderful medium. Its thick, opaque quality is good for overall use and for the building up of images. But tempera requires space, storage, and cleanup on a bigger scale than most other art materials. It's a rather demanding, unwieldy, and messy medium. One would need to start with five good-sized jars of it (for the primary colors—red, blue, and yellow—plus black and white), then transfer the paint to smaller containers. There are also the trays and the little coasters, the brushes, the water containers, and the sponges to consider. And one needs a big enough surface to work on. I think that using tempera at home would be a big production, but if you want to tackle it, more power to you.

What about other paints?

If you're getting into other paints, a little set of watercolors might be more manageable, and it's not too messy. Although watercolors don't compare with tempera in terms of flexibility and durability, they offer intrinsic pleasures for children who want to explore with a brush. Their general wateriness and floppy brushes, however, make this a difficult medium to control. Yet children, being as brilliant as they are, do find ways to work with them.

Aren't there other materials for painting as well?

Cray-Pas and Magic Markers are crossover materials, somewhere between drawing and painting. The Cray-Pas, which are very waxy crayons, have a painterly feeling to them. Many parents like to opt for these because they're so much more manageable than paint, although they too are somewhat messy.

What about pastels?

They are as messy as can be. Once a pastel falls on the floor, parents will permanently bar them from the house, after they buy a new rug. But kids like them, so they can be used out in the yard or on the back porch.

That pretty much limits the choices, doesn't it?

Not necessarily. One kind of paint that might work well at home is a simple set of acrylics. These paints come in tubes and are not expensive. Acrylics look very rich, like oil paint, and children can work and rework a painting with them. (We don't use acrylics at school simply because our tempera paints work so well.) Acrylics are sometimes available in beginner's sets. You need three tubes for the primary colors, plus black and white. (Many great artists have reduced their palettes to very few colors, yet have managed to get a whole range of hues out of them.) The tubes are squeezed out in small amounts on a paper palette. Children can use bristle brushes and mix the colors as they would the tempera paint. Acrylics dry rather quickly, so the brushes need to be cleaned right after they're used. With water-based acrylics, the cleanup is easy.

CLAY

Although I rotate the materials I offer the children, the one they cannot get enough of is clay. They never tire of this wet, wonderful, sticky material that will do anything they want. Their response is very deep. Perhaps it's because they spend their days with books, paper, pencils, and more paper. They love to touch the clay, to experience its sensuality.

Clay is the one material I have to hold back on. Even when I tell the kids that we're going to paint a mural the following week, they come into the art room and ask, "Aren't we doing clay today?" I patiently tell them, "You know you will do clay. Everyone in this school does clay. You will do clay a lot, but you cannot do it every week. We have to wait while the work of the other classes is being fired in the kiln." However, when the kids are really antsy, I might say, "Today we are doing clay."

The clay we use is an inexpensive variety that is gray before it's fired, but turns whitish afterward. Considering how inexpensive and deeply satisfying it is, I let the children have

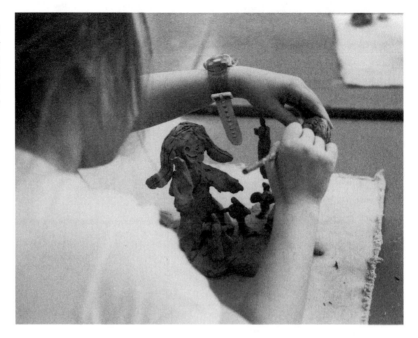

After modeling these figures and joining them to the base, this child uses a pin-tool to incise the texture of the hair

as much as they want. I buy it in quantities of five hundred pounds at a time. The clay comes in fifty-pound cardboard boxes, containing two plastic bags, each holding twenty-five pounds.

Note: Neither plasticine nor a self-hardening clay are as responsive to the touch as this natural clay, which can be fired in a kiln.

Of all the materials I offer, clay requires the least setting up in advance. Before the children arrive, I slice one of the boxes open, pull out a twenty-five-pound bag, and plunk it down on the bat (a clay table with a plaster surface that soaks up the moisture). I remove the plastic covering and, with a long length of wire, divide the clay into large chunks. Then I pull these chunks apart.

When I offer the children clay at the beginning of the class, I want it to be new from the maker or nicely reconditioned. I consider a fresh block of clay an aesthetic gift. I feel strongly about this. I know that some teachers spend a lot of time slapping the chunks of clay into balls in the belief that it's better for the children to start with a premade rounded shape. But I like the children to experience being the first to touch the freshly cut clay themselves. There's nothing like it.

Before the kids arrive, I have already plunked down a piece of canvas about the size of a place mat in front of every stool. The children will place their clay on the canvas to keep it from sticking to the table. (These rectangular cloths have

This five-year-old boy rolls out his coils of clay, then joins them to make an airplane

been in use in the art room for many years.) With the chunks of clay out and the canvas in place, I can start the class immediately.

When the kids enter and see the canvas mats in front of their stools, they know what's coming. They start shouting, "Clay! Clay!" and we're off and running. I hold them back for only a moment to say whatever needs to be said before they go at it.

The Nature of Clay

With the five- and six-year-olds, I begin by talking about the clay itself. We might talk about what clay is—how it's a mineral from the earth, made up mostly of feldspar. We might talk about how heavy it is, how soft it is, how responsive it can be to the fingers. I really don't need to say too much. I certainly wouldn't suggest to the little kids that they make some sort of an object with the clay. I want them to explore the material for themselves and to discover what it will do. There is nothing I can teach them that they won't learn by exploring the material themselves. They find out what clay is as soon as they get their hands on it: touching it, squeezing it, pounding it, poking it, patting it, pulling it apart, opening it up. I cannot say strongly enough that I see art as an exploratory process in which the material itself largely teaches the children.

After we've talked a little about clay (which we might do only on the first day) I will say to the younger kids, "This is clay. What would you like to do with it?" Or, "Today, I'd like to see what you would like to do with clay. How can you work with it?" Then I will ask them if they're ready to get their clay.

Children like to explore clay using both their hands and their tools

Suddenly the room becomes totally quiet. Everyone seems to be ready. I call on the kids one at a time. As a selection method, I may call first on those who were born in July and August, or call on them individually by name. They come racing over to the clay table. They estimate which chunk is the biggest and try to grab it. (They're all that way.) Then they sit down and start pounding the clay. Many of them only want to pound it for a long time. It's going to take them a year or two to even grasp the potential of this material. They will need that time to figure out the properties of clay for themselves.

I teach them that their hands are their best and most expressive tools. Young children, using only their hands, can make marvelous things. But some tools also have to be made available. The older children in particular like to have access to them. I offer them wooden modeling tools, pin tools, and wire tools. These are used respectively for shaping the clay and joining things together, marking textures, and hollowing out the pieces. The pin tool has an actual pin at one end, like a toothpick. The wire tool is shaped with a loop to hollow out the pieces so they can be fired in the kiln.

When the kids get their hands on these tools, they seem to regress for a while. They don't model as vigorously as they did before because they're busy playing with the tools. They often pound the tools into the clay. (You have to let them get some of this forceful activity out of their systems.) Sometimes the tool becomes part of the clay; the kids might, for example, use it as a flagpole. I will often pull back on the tools, but the kids eventually come to use them in moderation and to rely on their hands to a much greater degree.

At the beginning of the year, I teach the children how to clean up after class. They need to be taught to save their left-over clay for recycling, to put the canvas fabric and the tools away, and to clean up generally. (It's so hard for the kids to disengage from their work to do this, but if they didn't, I would have to do all the cleanup myself.)

Leftover Clay

The leftover clay is always reused. I recondition it until it's as fresh as the day it arrived. The children bring their unused clay over to the bat table and I pound and knock it about into a big chunk. Then I put a hole into it—with the handle of a mallet or something similar—to open it up. I fill the hole with water and seal it up by pinching the clay. I place the water-filled chunks in a large can lined with a plastic bag, sprinkle some water on top, and cover it all with the lid. The clay needs to sit about a week to be restored. Pouring too much water on the outside would make the clay slippy and slidey, but the water inside the ball makes it soft enough to be almost perfect.

Note: There are also many crumbs of clay left on the canvas mats. If the children picked their mats up casually, the crumbs would fall on the floor and there would soon be clay on the stairs and throughout the school. So I have the kids carefully carry their mats to the trash can and discard the crumbs there.

The children often see art class as a time to be social. Working with clay, in particular, is a highly social experience. Clay, being tactile as well as visual, somehow requires less direct attention. It frees up the children, giving them the most leeway to talk about other matters. They talk, talk, talk about things like the movie or the TV program they saw the previous day or week. While all this interaction is going on, they're still paying some attention to their work. The question I'm faced with is just how much conversation to allow. Of course, if the children are talking about what they're doing, I always permit that. Sometimes, however, I tamp down the discussion, particularly if it gets too loud. I might say, "For five minutes, we are not going to do any talking whatsoever, and I'll tell you when the five minutes are up." To signal the beginning of the silence, I look up at the clock and say, "Get ready, get set, and go." A lot of deep work gets done in those five minutes. Then I say, "The five minutes are up. If you want to talk now, talk quietly with your neighbor." By that time the kids are so deeply immersed in their work, they remain fairly quiet.

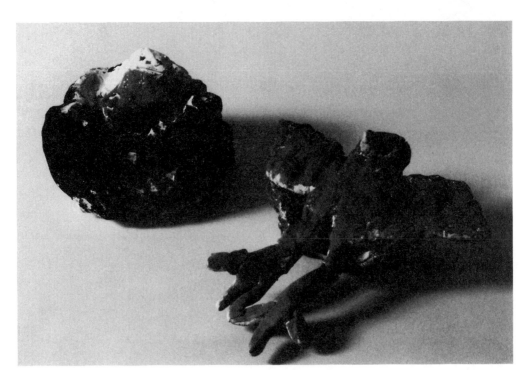

Two approaches to birds and their nests by five-year-olds. Claire focused on the nest itself, while Gaby concentrated on the bird

Narrative Play

The younger kids do a lot of narrative play with their clay, much like they do when playing with blocks. Gender differences also show up early here. The boys' play can include lots of crashing and exploding. The boys may, for example, make a tunnel and say, "The monster lives there." Or they may make an opening in a mound and say, "There are a lot of bad guys in here." Then the boys have to bomb the tunnel, so they put some clay on top to indicate the bomb before they demolish the tunnel. This is how a bunch of five- or six-year-old boys may operate. The little boys especially sit closer together to pound and work with the clay. They often do joint projects. They say, "Let's make a volcano," or something similar. So you let it happen. You have to let them engage in this social narrative play together. Finally, they will separate; they will go on to do pieces of their own.

The girls, on the other hand, seem to stroke their clay. Some will make nests, creating open vessel shapes and putting eggs in them. I might ask a girl, "Where is the bird?" as a way of suggesting she might develop her narrative work further.

Sometimes I intervene more directly. After observing one girl for a while and seeing that she made a nest but nothing further was happening, I took a small piece of clay, pressed two wings into the sides, pulled out a tiny beak, and set the bird at the edge of her nest. Some might consider such intervention highly intrusive, but I wanted to raise her level of interaction with the clay. In fact, the girl squealed with excitement. She immediately picked up the bird and flew it over to somebody else's nest nearby. When another girl who was watching asked me to make a bird for her too, I told her gently, "You know how to make your own bird now."

Note: There is actually more of a gender mix than I have indicated. Some of the younger boys and girls are best buddies and engage in many crossover activities, working on their clay together.

While the children are working, I walk around the room observing them. (I discourage them from bringing their pieces to me because I like to go around the room and talk about their work with them as it proceeds.) I feel it's a privilege to watch what the children are doing and get paid for it. I find myself looking on in wonderment as their individual and group dynamics play themselves out.

In talking with the children, I might say to one boy, "You dug all the way through. I can see all the way through the opening you made." Or, "I can see how your fingers make little marks on this side." And, "Over here, you've squeezed a wall up all around the edge." This might inspire the child to squeeze the wall all the way around. By describing something I see, I'm hoping to make them more conscious of their own activity. It's also my way of telling them that I am involved with what they are doing. It raises their own level of seriousness. They work hard. Play is hard work for children. They are learning at a rapid rate.

As the person supervising the children, I have to judge how long I want the kids to explore. I have to determine when the fruitfulness, and the learning and the value of playing and pounding around with the clay, is sufficient, and then I take them in a new direction. The next level is the object they will ultimately fire and take home. But first there's a long transition period.

A boy, for example, makes a long track or a road with his clay. I might make a small vehicle in clay, just a simple rectangular form that could serve as a train or a truck. I simply hand it to him without a word. In effect, I'm validating and reinforcing his efforts. I'm telling him I know where he's at, that I "get it." This takes the child's development to another level.

Working Figuratively

When the kids are six or seven, they begin to work more figuratively. They start modeling animals and people. If I give them some clay and say, "Make a ball of clay," most children try to make it into a ball. But they work right on the table, so it flattens on the bottom, taking the shape of a mound rather than a ball. I talk about making snowballs instead. When you ask the children to make a snowball, they start making it between their hands in the air, not on the table. Then I ask them to make the snowball into either a cigar or a sweet potato shape. So the kids squeeze the snowball a bit to make a longer shape. Then I say, "Choke the clay." When they do this, suddenly there's a head at the top of the cigar and that's pretty exciting.

I might demonstrate how to develop the figure further. I have the children watch me without any clay in their hands. I might roll out a piece of clay to show them how to do a little rolling, perhaps calling it a coil or not. Then I will break it in half and attach one section at the shoulders for each of the

After modeling an animal, this five-year-old boy adds texture marks to indicate the fur

arms. Using my fingers, I split the bottom part of the cigar shape into the two legs. Suddenly there's a simple figure of a person. Then right away I might just tip this figure over, bring the head up a bit and pinch the clay to form ears. Suddenly it becomes a four-legged animal. I do this in about a minute to show the kids that there's no magic involved in creating a figure, that it can be done quickly and simply.

I always stress the importance of joining the pieces of clay so the work will hold together. I tell the children, "If you put legs on the figure, you can't just push them into place and hope they'll stay there when the clay dries because they'll fall right off." I say, "Be vigorous. Go ahead and use your fingers to join those things." I talk about joining all the time. I talk about "smooshing" the clay, for lack of a better word. This involves pushing the clay into place, then pressing it firmly all the way around so that it will hold.

From the time the children are five or six, they need to understand that when two pieces are joined, they must stay together. My biggest job over the first few years is to show the children how to make their clay strong, viable, and resistant to breakage. I want to make sure that they don't produce piddley pieces, where everything breaks off after they leave the class. I really emphasize that. I feel it is important to retain the integrity of the material and show them how to make it work. I'm always going around the room to make sure that the clay parts they join are properly pressed together to make them strong.

Some teachers use a traditional scoring technique for joining pieces of clay. If a horse's leg is to be joined to its body, they first score the leg on both sides with a pin. Then, at the spot where it's to be joined, they rub in some slip (clay made liquid with water) and push the pieces together. The slip acts as a glue. I don't do this with sculpture, although I do use the slip technique with pottery. I've thought about this carefully. I have given the children clay that's moist and in perfect condition. I would rather see them push the pieces of this nice soft plastic clay together and then smoosh them. If there isn't enough clay to hold the pieces together, the kids can add some more and build it up that way. Using the slip in a brief art period can be a distraction and a detour, slowing down the children's sculptural growth. It not only interferes with their sense of form, but the watery slip can partially obliterate the sculptural surface and become a slippery end in itself.

The child who is least successful with clay is the one who makes the perfect cat head, very small and oh-so-perfect. However, perhaps by the time he or she has finished the perfect body and wants to join it to the head, both sections have become very dry. To join the head to the body, the kid is going to have to smoosh the head a little bit and that will change its shape. This induces panic in the child, who has made the perfect cat head. The children have to learn that they must first establish the general shape of the animal or the person before they can perfect the details.

Over time, the children learn about clay. They know what works and what doesn't. They learn to trust this material. They know that its heaviness may make a piece fall. Yet because they accept that weight, they're able to counteract it. A horse is an animal with very narrow legs, but the kids can make a horse stand up because they understand the nature of clay. With experience, the kids can make incredible things. By the time they're seven, eight, and nine, the kids are making horses, with themselves on horseback.

Standing figures modeled by eight- and nine-year-olds (Danny, Andrew, Neil, and David). They learned that a thick base is necessary to support a tall figure

Nine-year-olds Abeje and Margay modeled these female figures with their wide skirts in clay

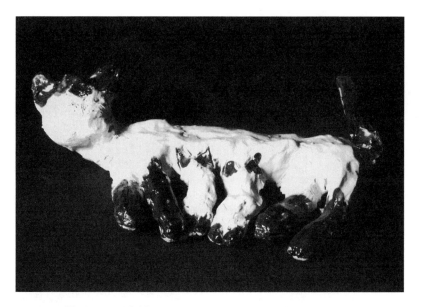

Ten-year-old Olivia modeled her Siamese cat and its nursing kittens in clay

They certainly understand about joining by then. If they don't, the pieces sometimes break. I let this happen because it's a great way for the kids to learn. I say, "Well, it broke because it didn't get joined right." As much as I hate for the work to fall apart, there's always the kid who doesn't do it properly, and that's the kid whose work I have to let fall apart.

If a child makes a cat and it's small, I might say, "Can you make the mother of that cat now?" When they show me that they can make a cat and make a bigger one as well, that connects them doubly with their work. I might even ask, "Do you want to nudge the two cats together, like they're cuddling? Would you like to join them as one piece of sculpture?" Very often the child will agree to do it. (We join the two by just going under the clay and squooshing them together a little bit.) I don't encourage the children to do bases for their sculpture because I think they will just use them to support little pieces. They figure that out often enough when the work

When I asked, "How do people show affection?" nine-year-old Matthew modeled himself in clay, petting his dog

seems weak. But I'm impressed when they make a flat piece to serve as the base and rescue a work that looks a little teetery. They will rest their piece on it and suddenly it holds together. I don't discourage that at all. It's great if it works. But I want them to be sure that the parts they join are pressed together to make them strong and solid.

What I discourage is toy making. By that I mean coming up with many little pieces that go together. A boy, for example, might want to make an aircraft carrier like the *Intrepid* (which is a floating museum docked on the Hudson River in New York), with as many little airplanes as will fit on the deck. I know this will never be a piece of sculpture, that all the little pieces will soon be broken and on the floor. I talk about the importance of having elements in the work that can be joined. I say, "We're here to make sculpture." On the bulletin board, I post many examples of free-standing sculptures, ranging from the ancient Greeks to Rodin, and modern works as well.

I will ask the children some questions so they can connect with their sculptures on a personal level. I might ask, "What do you like to do when you're sitting down?" Everybody then tells me. I say, "Well, you can make a seat with a bit of clay. Then what can you do?" I also ask them what they like to do when they're lying down, or feeling lazy, and ask them to

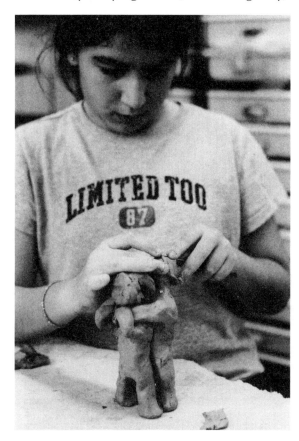

This nine-year-old girl dramatically expresses the idea of friendship by joining her two figures together

show that in clay too. I might also ask, "Can you think of a mother and her children?" Another idea is asking the children to do something that will stand on three legs, like a person with a hockey stick or a cane. Or asking, "How do animals show affection?"

I try not to rush the children's work, although I realize that when their spontaneity goes, they can lose their connection with the piece. Sometimes I will save a work-in-progress from one week to the next. Occasionally I might ask them to do something that must be finished in one period. I'll say, "Only one piece today and it's got to be finished by the end of the period." At first the children think that this is a real restriction, but it isn't at all. They get right into it. They're very ambitious; most of the older children are ambitious in clay.

Although my emphasis is on doing free-standing three-dimensional sculptures, there is also the world of ceramics, of making pinch pots, coil pots, and slab pottery (whose sections are held together with slip). There are some kids who just make bowls. That's what they like to do. But as a rule, we don't go in heavily for pottery, except in connection with their social studies. I think the children are much more expressive when they do their free-standing sculptures, and I always encourage them to approach their work from every angle, every view.

One year I asked a group of ten-year-olds who had been doing crowd scenes in their paintings if they could do a number of people as a group in clay. One boy did a world championship wrestling event. (He had done a wonderful painting on the subject.) He did a little ring with some wrestlers and the referee. He had posts at the four corners with holes in them, which proved helpful after the piece was fired because we could thread ropes through them. This gave the work a lively and realistic effect.

Other group sculptures depicted the kids and their families as they sat on their living room couches watching TV with their dogs. Some children have depicted rock bands and produced other complex pieces.

Most five-year-olds don't even know that clay can be made into objects and saved. They don't know and they don't care. They're doing the exploratory stuff. They're playing with the clay. Although they have put a certain amount of effort into their work, it isn't necessary to save everything. If I see a piece that I find extraordinary, however, I might set it aside to be fired. But for the most part, with five-year-olds, I don't tell them that their work can be fired.

When the children are about six, they often come to the point where they themselves recognize that they may have made something worth saving. They may say to themselves: *I can make something with this clay and save it.* They certainly begin to know that clay makes inordinately exciting objects, which they want to take home.

As soon as the children begin to realize they can save their pieces and create ones that they want to save, I have to figure out the year's schedule for using the kiln. I might say, "This week we won't save our pieces and next week we will." Or, "You may each choose a piece to save." I bisque everything we save, usually firing the work of a couple of classes at a time. (Bisque is a clay that has been fired but not glazed.)

Note: I never set any limits on size. The kids know they can work as large as they wish. But they also know that if they want to save pieces, these will have to fit into the kiln.

A shark modeled by eight-year-old Sam, who enjoyed getting his hands around a big piece of clay. The bulk of the piece was supported by setting it directly on the table

Hollowing the Clay

The children learn about the thickness of clay for successful firing. They often make very thick pieces at the start. I constantly tell them that if there's a pocket of air in that thick clay, it will heat up faster than the clay molecules, which can cause an explosion in the kiln, breaking up their piece and someone else's piece nearby as well. I teach the children to hollow out those pieces.

One kid made a skyscraper. He worked in a broad, expressive way. He had this big hunk of clay and we had to decide, as we always do: Do we keep it or not? Let's suppose we want to keep this one. Before the period is over we sit down together. I go in at the bottom with a wire tool to hollow it out, while the boy pulls the clay off the wire. We pull out the clay until I feel the thickness is not going to cause any problems. By the end of the period, I'm almost always able to hollow out the pieces for the children.

The children do some complex and extraordinary pieces; they will make a big figure like Darth Vader. You have to be careful about going into it and hollowing out the legs, for example. As the children watch me hollow, they begin to understand the problem. Ultimately, they're able to judge the right thickness for their clay and no longer make pieces that are cumbersome to hollow out.

I once watched an art teacher show the children how to make balls of clay and how to hollow them out before joining them to form people and animals. I thought this was doing last things first. The kids couldn't model their animals very vigorously because the hollowed-out pieces would collapse. I believe the whole pleasure of clay is going at it spontaneously. The technical details can be learned later.

When a piece is sufficiently hollow, I turn it upside down, write the child's first name on the bottom, and hand the work

When I asked, "How can you show people helping each other?" seven-year-old Vera modeled herself sick in bed at home, while her father brought her a bowl of chicken soup

to him, saying, "Put it on that shelf over there to dry." (The clay has to dry completely before it can be fired because any moisture would cause it to explode.) The children have to carry their work about twenty feet. I watch and see whether it can reach the shelf without falling apart; it's a test of the work's viability. If things fall apart on their way to the shelf, that indicates the pieces weren't joined well. It's a good lesson for the children to learn. Most of the time, the work remains intact.

Once dry, the clay is quite fragile. (After firing, it's nice and hard.) In its delicate state, a piece on the shelf should not be touched or handled. The thing that pleases me so much is that the kids in my school don't touch each other's work. They could, but they don't. They have so much respect for the work of others.

The younger children often paint their fired pieces with tempera. I wait until they have done clay for several weeks, get really good at it, and have completed a number of pieces. By then they can't wait to paint them; they love painting their work. The big day comes. When the children arrive in the art room, the paint trays are out. They can paint two or three of their clay pieces in one period. Fired clay is very absorbent and the tempera dries quickly, so the kids can work freely with color. They are heady with excitement. They think this is the best thing that has ever happened to them. (At other times, leaving their work unpainted helps them become more aware of its shapes and shadows.)

They love their painted clay pieces. They say, "Can we take them home today?" They can at the end of the period. Sometimes the children have too many pieces to carry, so I'll put them in a box and send them downstairs. Other times, I may take a whole series of animal pieces or whatever and display them on a shelf for a while.

Note: The children get back every clay piece that was fired, as well as every other piece of work (collages, paintings, drawings, etcetera) that they do in the art room.

Adding the Glaze

The older children—seven-, eight-, nine-, and ten-year-olds—sometimes glaze their work to give it color. We use safe, lead-free, low-fire glazes that give the work a shiny, glassy surface, making it look special. I provide a wide variety of these glazes. The colors in their liquid state don't correspond to the colors after firing. (They look pastel-like. For example, a wet blue glaze will look pale pink.) So I set out sample tiles to show the children how the finished color will appear. And I always remind the children *not* to put any glaze on the underside of their work because it will turn to glass and stick to the shelf of the kiln.

Clay can also be used for wall plaques done in high relief and low relief. I might ask a group of eight- and nine-year-olds about an animal they once saw. Maybe they played with a dog or a cat. Maybe they rode a horse. The idea would be for them to do the subject on a clay pancake, like an animal cracker. Of course, there will always be the kid who didn't see any animals, so I will say to him or her, "Is there any animal that you like or have read about?"

Then I'll talk about doing the animal in low relief because I visited a tile factory and found a wonderful little tile with a bird in relief. I'll explain that they could easily make a raised-

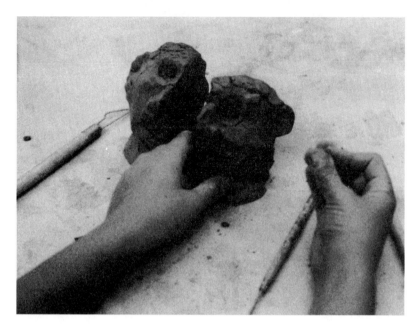

This nine-year-old boy sees friendship as separate individuals who are of one mind

up animal on top of the pancake just by adding bits of clay and joining them well. We might do it in red clay, glaze it, then take some of the glaze off the raised part with a sponge so the animal itself would appear as raw red clay. This would be a tightly focused project with a specific result as its objective, which is something I don't often do. By cutting a slot out of the back, we can hang the plaque on the wall with a nail.

Note: I started using red clay for special projects when we were making Greek pottery and decorating it in red and black. For tile making, I have experimented with red clay mixed with grog (small fired-clay particles), which is different in its strength and texture. I try new things all the time. I'm always adding ideas and materials to my teaching repertory.

Another clay plaque project, which was demanding, involved the nine- and ten-year-olds, who had been concentrating on Greece in their social studies class. They were making charcoal drawings of the figure. So I told one child, "You are Artemis"; another, "You are Apollo"; and so on. The kids acted out a scene from a Greek myth, and at its most dramatic moment I said, "Freeze." They then drew each other in charcoal as action figures. The following week, they selected their favorite drawing, transferred it to a clay plaque, and developed it as a bas-relief. (They had studied ancient Greek clothing and had some sense of the drapery.) The plaques were then fired and left unglazed.

FOR PARENTS

Parents who'd like their kids to work with clay at home have asked:

Is working with clay important for children?
Yes. It not only lets them work in three dimensions but can be a factor in their development. Since young children seem to need to go through the process of playing with mud, clay is certainly a great step above that.

What about the children who don't feel comfortable about putting their hands in clay?
There are those rare children who don't like to touch clay. When that occurs, I suggest that you might make your child more receptive by kneading and making bread with her or by having her form the meatballs for spaghetti and meatballs. You might also try using Play-Doh as an alternate material. Although this doesn't come close to working with clay, it does

provide that wonderful process of patting and pounding and getting your hands in it.

What types of clay would you suggest?

There is nothing like natural clay, which is cheap and readily available. But natural clay presents a number of problems for use at home. For one thing, it comes in twenty-five-pound bags, and the minimum order may be fifty pounds. Some workshops that make clay pots on a potter's wheel might sell it to the public in smaller amounts.

Natural clay also needs to be kept moist, as has been described in this chapter. It can then last for several years. Success with this material depends in part on how much maintenance you are willing to give it.

Is it necessary to save the pieces in clay?

The age of the child is relevant here. When children are four, five, and six, they don't know anything about "saving" clay and are generally content with the process itself. As they get older, the results become important to them and they want to save their pieces. When the work dries, it is so fragile that the pieces must be placed out of reach or they need to be fired. Most people don't have access to a kiln, however. Since pottery workshops have kilns, parents with access to them might be able to get their children's work fired there.

What about cleanup problems with clay?

Parents may think that natural clay is messy, but it actually isn't. Although the children's hands will be covered with a powdery white clay, it can be rinsed right off at the sink. The rest of the clay can easily be rolled back into a ball, then stored (as has been previously described) in its container.

What about alternatives to natural clay?
There are self-hardening clays and plasticine. The self-hardening clay dries hard and is less fragile than natural clay. Although plasticine provides less malleability than the natural clays, it doesn't dry out, so it can be reworked and reused. The plasticines now on the market come in individually wrapped blocks sold in different quantities. They are also available in as many as six or eight bright, beautiful colors.

This six-year-old girl got some paint for her sponge; she then tapped it onto the stencil with its cut-out flower shapes

PRINTMAKING

I do printmaking with children of all ages, starting with the five-year-olds. Sometimes a young child will discover the idea for himself. Somehow, some way, a five-year-old in the painting class will find that tapping a paint-laden sponge on paper makes a series of repeated marks or patterns. (The thing about printing is its wonderful possibility to repeat.) The children get excited about this. So when spontaneous sponge-tapping occurs, I let it run on for a bit, although I don't particularly want to emphasize it. I like to keep the painting class as a painting class.

Note: The two ten-year-old girls who wanted to create the effect of water in their painting class, as described earlier, used their sponges deliberately. Setting their brushes aside, they dipped their sponges in paint and produced the desired watery effect with a repeated up-and-down tapping. Other spontaneous forms of printmaking are fingerprints and handprints. The younger kids take great pleasure in making their own impressions of these.

Creating Plates and Stamps

Formalized printmaking calls for plates and/or stamps. The plates carry inscribed or raised images, which are inked and then transferred to paper. (I use the term *plate* even with five-year-olds and explain that what holds the image is called the plate.) We employ various materials in platemaking. These include Styrofoam (an easy version of the woodcut), linoleum blocks, and sturdy cardboard for collographs. We make some stamps ourselves, and we also use found objects, such as plastic forks, bottle caps, and empty spools of thread. We make various rubbings too, and do decorative patterns by printing on clay. We use stencil printing as well to produce repeated images. The children do a simple drawing on paper here, such as a flower. I put a small rectangle of see-through stencil paper over each drawing and then cut the image out with an X-Acto knife. (The older children can cut their own stencils.) The colors are tapped in with small sponges and tempera paint.

Our simplest printing plate is made of Styrofoam. I started out using the Styrofoam trays that come with the shrink-wrapped fruit and meat from the supermarket. I cut the edges off with scissors and set the trays aside until I saved about twenty-five of them, which I then distributed to the children. I told them, "You'd better not make a mistake on this because every child gets just one." When there was a mistake, the kid would turn the tray over to use the other side and see numbers on the bottom. When they said they didn't like using the other side, I told them, "You get only one . . ." Styrofoam sheets can now be bought in art-supply stores, which make this material available by the box.

In demonstrating printmaking with the Styrofoam plate, I first draw an image with simple broad lines, using a dull pencil rounded at the end. I press the pencil hard to get the lines incised deeply into the surface. The next step is to ink the plate. Squeezing a little printer's ink onto a piece of twelve-by-twelve-inch double-ply glass, I roll out the ink, spreading it on the glass with a soft, spongy rubber brayer or roller about three or four inches wide. (When the ink is evenly distributed, it feels kind of tacky; you can even hear a tacky sound.) After I roll the ink evenly onto the Styrofoam plate, I carefully lower a sheet of paper over it, making sure it drops down evenly. With the paper in place, I rub the back of it gently by hand to transfer the inked image to the paper. I then lift the paper off, "pulling" the print.

Note: The sheet of paper is always somewhat larger—by about three inches—than the printing plate, so that it will extend over the

When I asked, "How can you use stencils and tempera paint to make a garden?" nine-year-old Sydney used variations and repetitions, then used a brush to add the stems and leaves (16" × 18")

edge. For example, a five-by-seven-inch plate calls for a sheet of paper that's eight by ten inches.

Once I see that the five- and six-year-olds are doing simple line drawings of people or animals, I suggest that they do a direct drawing on the Styrofoam plate and we can then print it. (Sometimes they like to do their sketches on paper first to get an idea for a drawing.) Their image may be a simple animal with a head, four legs, and a generalized shape. With older, more skilled children, the animals are more specific and can readily be identified as a porcupine, lion, moose, or buffalo. The subject matter may also come from the children's favorite sports or from the books they're reading. When the kids have completed their Styrofoam plates, I write their names on the backs with permanent markers to help identify the prints they will make.

The little kids are excited when we pull their prints; they squeal with delight at seeing them. Once they observe the process, they go into high gear. They run over to do another one. They cannot believe that the image repeats, that they can see it over and over again—they think that they have to draw another picture. I say, "No, you just ink it. You just go and re-ink it." Once the kids get the knack, they run back and make many prints from a single plate.

Separate Tables

I set up separate tables for the inking and the printing. Organizing them in this way helps to give the children a sense of clarity about the printmaking process. On the inking table, which I cover with newspaper, I set out four pieces of glass, tubes of

Julia, age seven, showed herself feeding her fish in this Styrofoam print (4½ × 6")

City scenes are depicted in these Styrofoam prints (4″ × 6″) made by Maya, above, and Charlie, opposite, both age nine

printing inks, and several brayers or rollers. (Although tempera paint can also be used, I find that the texture and viscosity of printer's ink makes for somewhat cleaner prints.) On the printing table, I set out stacks of paper in different colors. These are related in size to the size of the plate used that day and they allow for about a three-inch margin all the way around.

Note: Printer's ink comes in both tubes and cans, but I prefer the tubes, having found that in a few months the ink in cans may dry out.

As soon as the kids have done a print or two in one color, they invariably ask, "Can I change the color?" I say yes be-

cause I have restricted the inks I offer in a single session to those of similar value. One day I use only dark colors—black and blue; another day, hot colors—orange, red, and pink. Another time, I'll offer them white, gold, and silver. If the children had jumped from dark blue to orange, they would soon be muddying the inks. Had I put out opposite colors, I would constantly be admonishing them not to go to the yellow because they have just used the black, and so on.

After the children have inked their plates, they carefully carry them over to the printing table. We usually start out with plain white newsprint, which is what I use for my demonstrations. The kids use the newsprint until they begin to get a feeling for how the ink settles into the Styrofoam plate and how much ink to use. Later, we move on to special printing papers, which are thin and smooth, but tough. Those papers also come in bright colors. (The girls love magenta; that's the one they invariably choose.) Some of the papers have the same color on both sides; others are white on one side and colored on the other. The children often lower their paper onto the plate white side down, although they want to use the colored side. After making this mistake a few times, they realize they have to turn the sheet over. Sometimes I make a Japanese rice paper available and tell the children that when they get really good at printing, I will give them this good-quality material.

Drying the Papers

The logistics of drying the papers after printing are complicated. Printer's ink can take as long as a day to dry; the prints can get very sticky. There are hundreds of them and they can't be placed one on top of another. So we lay them out on large sheets of construction paper—six or so to a sheet—and slide them onto a shelf or rack to dry overnight.

Collographs

In addition to the Styrofoam, another kind of printing process the children frequently use is the collograph. This consists of a heavy piece of cardboard or railroad board (a thick, heavy-ply, hard gray cardboard), onto which something is glued to create a raised surface. The addition is usually a softer cardboard—like men's shirt cardboard—which is easily cut with scissors. I try to keep everything on the plate gray so as not to confuse the children, but even if the cardboard is colored, the kids can see that it will become one color when it's inked.

For subject matter, I ask the eight- or nine-year-olds, "How can you cut shapes that show what you like to do in the winter?" For example, if a child went sledding, he might cut out the shape of his sled. Or the subject might be about the city, or about their social studies.

When I asked, "Did anyone fly anywhere this summer?" Patrick, age nine, did this collograph of a rhinoceros beetle which can fly (9" × 10")

After the children have cut out their images, scenes, or designs from the lighter-weight cardboard, I stress the importance of not overlapping the pieces when they glue them onto the heavier cardboard. I also stress getting enough glue in the corners and under the edges. When the gluing is done, I ask the kids to put their plates facedown, then to sit on them and count up to sixty. By that point, everything has been securely flattened out and the collographs are ready for their inking and printing.

For the five- and six-year-olds, it's particularly important to have them print on the same day. This way they really understand the process. Should a whole week go by, they would lose the connection between platemaking and printing, and you can't expect them to figure it out. This is why I have the younger children sit on their collographs for sixty seconds. It makes the glue hold well so they can do their printing on the same day. The next time, the children may be willing to go slower because by then they will have understood the process. (When using Styrofoam, the children can easily draw, ink, and print from the plates they make on the same day.)

For the collographs, instead of gluing only the lighter cardboard onto the heavier cardboard, we can add other materials for textural effects. Netting, burlap, and lace, among others, can be arranged on the plate and glued down. All the children enjoy exploring the effects these textures produce when the plates are printed.

Rubbings

Before making any prints from their collographs, the children can use them for rubbings. They simply place a piece of white newsprint over the surface of the plate and, with a wax crayon, rub across it in even strokes to pick up the image. I use dark crayons, removing the paper coverings and snapping them into short, stubby two- or three-inch pieces. The children use the sides of the crayons, not the points, for their rubbings. After doing several of these, they can take their collographs to the inking table and proceed to make prints from the same plates.

The children find the rubbing technique fascinating and use it in many ways. Coins are a particular favorite. Using newsprint and crayons, they can also rub the texture of the radiator in the classroom, bricks, a rattan chair. The children love to scoot around outside the art room and find different textures to bring back. They can easily do a score of different rubbings from objects found in the school. The kids also do rubbings of the bottoms of their sneakers, which have deep, embedded patterns. They think their sneakers are fantastic—the very best thing in the world for rubbings.

I sometimes give kids a special demonstration to show them that if an object has enough—but not too much—of a raised surface, it can be "read" on a print. I have brought a fresh fish to school, rolled ink across its surface, then placed a piece of white newsprint over the fish and rubbed it gently. When I pulled the paper off, the surface texture of the scales and the exquisite way in which they overlap could be seen. This is a dramatic way of showing that there are all kinds of surface textures. It's also a wonderful way of sensitizing children to the world around them. (The kids who observed the fish demonstration did not, however, repeat it themselves.)

Linoleum Blocks

With the eight- and nine-year-olds, I introduce linoleum block printing. I don't do this with younger children because sharp tools are required. Each child puts his or her linoleum block on a jig. The jig is a twelve-by-twelve-inch piece of plywood with thin strips of wood attached at either end—one to the top surface, the other to the bottom. The bottom piece hooks over the table, stabilizing the jig, while the top piece keeps the linoleum block from shifting. As they work, the children brace the linoleum against the top strip. With the tools, they also cut in that direction, away from themselves. I always remind them not to direct the knife toward their hands.

This ten-year-old boy carves a landscape image into his linoleum block with one hand while holding the block down with the other

Ten-year-old Erica did a linoleum print showing a boat on choppy water at camp with three figures in motion (6" × 9")

Note: To make the linoleum easier to work, the blocks can be set briefly on a radiator in cold weather to soften them. At other times, a very hot iron is useful, with a piece of fabric placed on the linoleum block for protection and the block heated for less than a minute. (The linoleum can be rewarmed later, if necessary.)

We did linoleum prints influenced by the Japanese approach to wood blocks. We had gone to an exhibition of Japanese prints and studied how these were made. One of our related projects was based on the work of a specific printmaker, who had created a great number of views of one mountain in Japan. The children were going to do twenty-six views of the World Trade Center in lower Manhattan. (Their classroom teacher and I had jointly worked up this assignment.)

Following the Japanese style, we made drawings on the linoleum blocks, then cut away everything else but the lines, which would print black, because we used black ink here. The

Kate, age ten, showed a street vendor in this 5" × 5" linoleum print. The scene and its rhythms are a balance of black and white areas

cut-away areas would appear as white. We did not do the colors in the Japanese style because that would have involved a number of separate plates. (The Japanese make a different wood block for each color.) Instead, we shortcut the process. First, we made a plate of just the black lines—the linear part of the image—and printed up a number of copies. The kids then took a weak print and used it as a guide to transfer the black lines onto a separate Styrofoam plate. Then they cut the Styrofoam into several sections, depending on the image: the sky area, the land area, and so on. They inked these separately with different colors and—turning them upside down—carefully fitted them back into the spaces between the black-inked lines of their good prints. They gently rubbed the paper underneath until the colored ink came off the Styrofoam. The work was technically demanding, but it produced splendid results.

We went to the Brooklyn Botanic Garden at cherry blossom time to sketch the trees. When the children returned to school they drew these on linoleum blocks in the Japanese style, by cutting away everything but the lines. The work was complicated and intense, but the children were relaxed and produced beautiful work.

Stamp Printing

We make our own stamps for stamp printing, utilizing various and readily available materials. We sometimes use potatoes. After slicing them in half, we cut some texture or a design into their exposed surfaces with the end of a paring knife. We tap the potato onto a tray of ink and then stamp it on paper. We have used fruit too, cutting oranges and apples in half and using dome-shaped carrot tops as well, inking them to make interesting prints. We have also used large rectangular erasers, by carving a motif or design into one end of the cube, then inking and making prints from it. A favorite material is the dense spongy rubber padding used under rugs. To make a stamp here, we cut a simple shape out of the rubber, then glue it onto a little chunk of wood about two inches square. We use Elmer's glue, which takes a while to dry, so the children can't make their stamps and print with them on the same day. The nine- and ten-year-olds can take the full class time for just making their complicated stamps.

We have used found objects, like bristle blocks, which are plastic rectangles with lots of little teeth that enable them to interlock. (They are the precursors to Lego blocks.) The bristle blocks, which are great for printmaking and for texturing clay as well, can be found among children's discarded toys. I have even gone into classrooms that have an abundance of such toys, found one or two that are cracked, and asked the teacher, "Could I just have one of these?" Or, "Would you mind giving this one up permanently?"

The stamp-printing idea is wonderful for the five- and six-year-olds. When they come into the room, I might offer them two or three things they can stamp with. I provide these children with tempera paint, not printer's ink. I put out red or blue paint on a tray, along with a few simple stamp makers. These might be Legos and bristle blocks, or some premade stamps with geometric shapes or circle designs.

I might ask the children, "How would you like to stamp these on a piece of paper?" The first thing the kids will do is to stamp very randomly all over the paper. Then I might ask, "Can you make a pattern with them?" The children find their own ways in which their stamping can make repeat patterns.

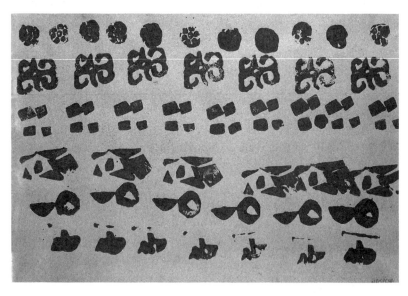

Using several stamps inked with tempera, five-year-old Natasha repeats each motif in its own line on construction paper (12" × 18")

Eight-year-old Anna incised a geometric design on a Styrofoam rectangle, glued it to a small block of wood, then used printer's ink to stamp the repeats (5½" × 6"). New patterns were created by rotating the block

It is a social experience for them as well, because they share their stamps with one another.

In printing, the image is reversed. The children see the prints of their little animals coming up in reverse and have to adjust to that fact. Kids who want to use words in their work have to learn to write backward. They write the words on a piece of paper, turn the paper over, and hold it up to the window. They can then retrace the letters on the back.

I'm against having children use words and letters in the art room. But one girl apparently needed to do some lettering, so I let it pass. She did a linoleum block that featured a big tube of Crest toothpaste. She wrote the letters backward, cut them out, transferred them from the paper to her linoleum block, and made her print. She pulled it off beautifully. Other kids will include the numbers that appear over the entry doors of their apartment buildings.

I downplay and discourage lettering in printmaking (as I do in other art activities) because I see the art room as a place where the children can be free to think with another part of their brain, to express themselves visually, in ways other than with words. To get their ideas across, they need to use images, colors, shapes, and lines.

The basic nature of printmaking is its capacity for repetition. I always try to think of ways in which making many prints would be a good thing. When I do printmaking, it's with the idea of not getting just one or two prints, but making an edition of six, seven, eight, or more. One autumn, the children made many little prints, which we mounted on small cards, put in envelopes, and sold at the book fair that the school holds at holiday time.

The children can also make paper for gift wrapping. Building up all-over patterns can make for beautiful papers for the holidays. The children can stamp their papers with little stars, using both gold and silver ink. One year, with the older children, we did snowflakes whose structure consisted of six ribs with elaboration. We cut them out of the rubber rug padding with scissors. After the snowflake shapes were glued onto wooden cubes, we stamped them with white paint onto dark blue and black paper. There were snowflakes all over the place. It was beautiful and we had tremendous fun doing this.

We also do printing on clay to decorate the ceramic cups or mugs we make. The stamps here are made of small, casually shaped clay pieces whose bottom surfaces are carved with a design. When fired, the clay pieces become sturdy and hard enough to be used as stamps.

I showed the children a book of Central American motifs derived from older pottery objects. Each child chose a simple motif from the book—a bird in flight, a flora or fauna. First, they shaped clay cylinders, then carved their images into one end of the cylinder or else into its side. The clay was then fired. The idea was to have the children print their flower or bird motifs along the edge of a long, rectangular slab of clay that would eventually become the cup or mug. The kids first rolled the soft, moist clay out flat, then used a cardboard template to establish the size of the rectangle. The previously made images carved into the cylinders were then stamped into the rectangular slab of wet clay. Or the carved cylinders were rolled across the slab of clay, repeating the image as they went along. The kids then picked up the long clay rectangle and joined its ends to form the cup or mug. They cut a round disk of clay to fit its diameter and joined this to the top. (Although the disk would serve as the bottom, it is easier to join it at the top and turn the piece over.) The cup or mug, with its imprinted motif running around the outside edge, was then fired in the kiln.

FOR PARENTS

Parents who wonder if printmaking is possible at home have asked:

Can children do printmaking at home?

Most parents think of printmaking as an adult activity. They don't realize that their kids can do it too. It's fun to do around the kitchen table at home, where the whole family can participate in this.

Do you need special equipment?

The only special items you need are a small roller to roll out the ink and the ink itself. These can be found in any art-supply store. The children can roll the ink out on a paper plate and throw the paper plate away when they are done. They can also use acrylic paint, which dries faster than ink.

What sorts of prints can the children make at home?

They can do potato prints and carrot prints, using a small knife. For stamp printing, they can carve an image, like a snowflake, on an eraser. The kids can also make collograph prints by cutting a little scene out of cardboard with scissors. Styrofoam prints are also fine at home; you can save the trays from supermarket meats for these. Your child makes the drawing on the tray; you can help with the incising if necessary.

How can the whole family participate?

Printmaking is a wonderful thing to do at holiday time, when many parents send out images of their children's work. Since printmaking is about repeating, you can easily make your own cards at home and make them in quantity. You can also do seasonal cards, for example, for Christmas, Easter, Rosh Hashanah, and Valentine's Day. The whole family can participate here.

CONSTRUCTION

In our construction activities, we build, primarily with boxes and other kinds of cardboard. (Because our school has a separate woodshop, we don't use wood in the art room, except in a peripheral way.) Our construction materials include corrugated cardboard—both one-sided and two-sided—oak tag, newspaper, and papier-mâché, along with glue, masking tape, wooden skewers, lengths of wire, and pipe cleaners.

Cardboard Boxes
We use all sorts of cardboard boxes. I save big boxes, medium boxes, long boxes, and little boxes. At home, I have a large plastic bag hanging over a doorknob near the kitchen in which to collect them. Carrying them to school makes traveling a bit bulky, but nevertheless worthwhile. I also have my colleagues at school save boxes for me. Even my mother-in-law saves them.

I look for boxes that are strong and sturdy, with a neutral

surface (not cluttered with a lot of lettering). I avoid those that are thin or floppy. I know a good box when I see one. For example, tubes of oil paint come in nice long white boxes that can be used for wonderful constructions. If I could easily get to school from an art-supply shop, I'd bring back a Santa Claus bag filled with such boxes. Other great boxes are the tall, square kind that liquor comes in and round sturdy ones, like those used for salt or for Quaker oats.

At school, I store the boxes away in plastic milk crates, which I keep at the edge of the room. I sometimes put the small square boxes in one crate, the larger square boxes in another, and the round ones in a third. I keep the miscellaneous sizes in plastic bags.

Like boxes, corrugated cardboard is great for construction activities. The two-sided corrugated is totally flat on both sides with a grooved or ribbed layer in between. It is brown or buff in color. A variant that is flat on one side and ribbed on the other comes in a number of bright, attractive colors. When cut vertically (along its grooves), the latter type doesn't curl up as much and stays rigid when it's set upright.

Note: Some of this corrugated cardboard comes from packing boxes with the word FRAGILE *stamped on them. I don't use the sections with lettering since that might distract the children. Many packing boxes come sealed with clear tape, which must be pulled off because glue will not stick to these areas when the work is assembled.*

Before the children arrive, I set out an assortment of boxes on a table, perhaps placing the round ones together in one group and the square ones in another so as to present them with a certain clarity. When the kids walk into the room and see them, they get quite excited. They know they'll soon be getting their hands on the construction materials. There isn't any age group that doesn't immediately respond in this way. I've already captured their interest just by putting the boxes out where they can see them. I have to restrain them until I can say a word or two about what we'll be doing that day.

In addition to the boxes, other construction staples are the cardboard tubes that come in rolls of both paper toweling and toilet tissue. Neutral gray in color and extremely adaptable, these can be stood up as columns or rolled as wheels. They can be left as they are or cut into smaller segments. When the children are asked how they want to combine these cylinders with some strong wonderful boxes, they are raring to go.

I let the young kids—the five- and six-year-olds—build without any kind of goal. I will ask them how they want to put some boxes together. Instead of having to make anything, they can just work with the shapes of the boxes. I might say to one child, "You've used three square shapes. Would you like to put a round shape with them?" Or, "Do you want to go up a little higher?" The children are discovering the properties of the material and learning the mechanics. They are finding out that if you put a heavy box alongside another box and try to glue it in place, it will slide right down. So they begin to get the idea of gravity. (The heavy box needs better support, and eventually, with my help, they learn how to accomplish this.) But basically I let the young children do their serious early play that involves discovering and learning. It is really the material here that's teaching the child.

With the older kids the eight- and nine-year-olds—I might corral them at the door, saying, "You can see we have a lot of three-dimensional materials in the room today." I tell them, "Choose a few of these and think about how you might want to put them together to make a vehicle or an animal." Or, "Maybe you just want to make a design with your boxes and will find some interesting shapes that go together."

I don't limit the number of boxes that any child can take. I never want to say, "Don't use more than five." I hate to limit the children, even though collecting all those boxes takes a lot of time and effort. There just might be a kid who will do something amazing with fifteen boxes. I remember one boy who was a remarkable builder from the time he was five. (When I mentioned this to his classroom teacher, she said, "He's the same way with blocks.") That child built the World Trade Center, along with the connecting bridges and columns and roadways. He fit things together so that everything was strong. He was a natural architect. Why would I want to stop a kid who was working that hard and on such an ambitious scale?

On the other hand, if I think a child is getting out of control and grabbing too many boxes for selfish reasons, I will intervene. You can see when a kid is not paying attention to his structure. If his first three boxes haven't held together, why would the next five hold? So I'll step in and set limits for that child.

Strong Joinings

A lot of construction involves joining. I always emphasize the importance of making strong joinings, of building strong structures. I convey to the children the idea that you want to make something that will hold together and not fall apart. The

Animals constructed by six-year-olds, using cardboard boxes and tubes

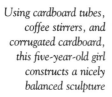
Using cardboard tubes, coffee stirrers, and corrugated cardboard, this five-year-old girl constructs a nicely balanced sculpture

underlying question they face is how to join the various elements without using cellophane tape, which is the adhesive they are the most familiar with. They have such tape at home and they think it's the only way to join things. But we don't use cellophane tape in the art room. It tends to be flimsy. Its slick surface doesn't take paint very well. We use masking tape instead, because it's generally stronger and provides a better surface to hold paint. To get the kids started, I often precut the masking tape before they arrive. I cut a roll into two-inch lengths and put the strips around the room—on the shelves, radiators, and the edges of the tables, where the kids have easy access to them. This can all be done really fast.

Sometimes the kids will put some tape on their constructions, expecting it to hold, and it doesn't. So we have demonstrations and discussions about this. There are always kids who try to join two boxes by using the narrow part of the tape (its width, rather than its length), so that half is on one side and half is on the other, while not really holding either. (The tape generally comes right off.) I could never understand the reason for this until I realized that the children didn't like the look of the tape and thought it would mar the surface of their boxes. They were trying to keep it from showing. They didn't realize, however, that once the construction was painted, the tape wouldn't show. When I explained this to them, their joinings became stronger.

We often use glue in combination with the tape. I tell the kids, "Elmer's glue is slidey, so don't use too much of it." I make the glue available in baby food jars here, as I do for collage. I also supply the same soft, cheap, skimpy little brushes they employ for collage.

If heavy construction is involved, the children can use the larger glue brushes with their dense bristles, but the smaller, softer brushes are usually sufficient for the job. I tell the kids that combining the glue with masking tape will make a particularly strong joining. I might say, "This box is kind of big and the glue may not hold. So if you position half the length of the tape across one box and half the length on the other, that will hold it while the glue dries." I tell them the joining will be really tight and will really hold if they allow it to dry for a bit.

In joining the various elements together, we use tabs as well as masking tape and glue. A tab is a piece of cardboard, about as long as a Band-Aid, that is folded in the

*Two constructions
by Evan and John,
both age five.
Employing various
materials, they
showed a grasp of
spatial relationships,
and also the use of
small forms to create
larger ones*

middle. (The tabs can also be made of oak tag or a heavy paper.) When glue is applied to both sides, the tab acts like a brace or a bracket to strengthen a joint, or to anchor a corner. The tabs make possible a lot of strong and stable building.

At the end of the period we try the "upside-down test," gently inverting a piece to make sure nothing falls off. The children like doing this test, particularly when their pieces hold together.

Our constructions often begin on a cardboard base. The bases are made of either heavy gray railroad board or corrugated cardboard, cut about ten inches square. One day when the kids walk in, I'll have a base cut for each of them, sitting in front of their seats. There is a lot of construction possible on a ten-inch square. You can put shapes together. You can build in space. You can build practically anything you want to.

The work the children do here might be a design or a fortification, a castle or a tower. I may show them pictures of such structures, with their crenellated walls. To build their castles the children may set on the base a circle of one-sided corrugated cardboard, which works particularly well for

A park scene constructed on a cardboard base by six-year-old Claire. The strip attached to the tree represents the sky, and the circle glued onto the strip represents the sun

curved forms. The one-sided corrugated cardboard curves easily and so is particularly good for castles and towers. It has other advantages too, since its grooves can hold wooden skewers, and coffee stirrers, toothpicks, paper straws, pipe cleaners, and wire. Things can rise from these grooves and go off in all directions.

Light wooden skewers are particularly useful here. Designed for cooking shish kebab and other barbecued foods, they are from three to twelve inches long. A stack of them can be purchased for a couple of dollars. Putting the wooden skewers in the corrugated grooves adds support to the structure, allowing the kids to build more than one level. The skewers hold really well in the corrugated cardboard. The

Two constructions made by nine- and ten-year-olds, using cardboard tubes, flat pieces, and coffee stirrers. The one on the left stresses symmetry; the one on the right achieves its own balance

A circular paper construction representing a Jacuzzi, made by six-year-old Gabby, who put herself in the whirlpool

same effect can be achieved with toothpicks, but they do best with some glue. I tell the children, "If you want things to be firm, you can dip your toothpick in the glue before you slide it into the ridges of the cardboard." The various building materials we use suggest all kinds of ideas. For example, the wooden skewers or wires can hold little flags.

Sturdy and flexible oak tag is another important construction material. I make it available as strips that I cut into various widths and keep in separate boxes. With these, the children can make arches, bridges, and other structures. I show them how to make a little flap, a kind of tab, at either end of the strip. This is done by scoring the oak tag (pressing the point of the scissors into it, giving it a nice place to bend), then applying a little glue to the flap to hold up the arch or whatever. (Another way to join the strips to the base is by stapling them.)

This six-year-old boy sets straws both inside and outside his sturdy cardboard tube

To create a bridge, the arched strip can be made flat on top by folding two corners into it to form an open rectangle. Anchored to the base, this then serves as the bridge. Because things go over bridges, the children might attach a strip of oak tag to make a road connected with the bridge and set little trucks on top. Because things go under bridges, the children can send little barges sailing below. I might show the children photographs of bridges and construction sites, boats, and similar things to stimulate their imagination.

We often talk about the city. The city is a big, big subject, and the kids can work on cityscapes. They can build their buildings with oak tag. I tell them that it might also be fun to design a park where they can play. I'll ask them, "How would you like to play in the park?" "What kind of equipment can you build?" I'll say, "There are things you climb up and things you slide down." Or, "How do you get up there? Well, build some stairs." I show the children pictures of ladders and demonstrate some of the folding techniques found in origami and similar books. I really don't have to show the kids that much. I often find that less is more because they come up with so many great solutions of their own.

Note: I see my job as teaching the children how to use the materials, but not what to do with them. I want them to come up with their own ideas. And invariably they do.

As the class period comes to an end, I have the children look at both their work and that of their classmates. I say, "Let's everybody look." I take their constructions to another table with a lazy Susan on it. The children want to spin the lazy Susan, but I ask them to stand back while I rotate the work slowly so that it can be viewed from various angles. We talk about each piece. I might say:

- You've repeated three circle shapes.
- Look how this one swings way up on both sides.
- Everything is on the inside.
- You've got this long shape in between.
- Everything seems to be shooting upward.
- You've got something hanging and it has this feel to it.
- This is a quiet interior space.

The children also describe what they see and become really excited about their work.

Working Together

Seven- and eight-year-olds can sustain an interest in their construction activities week after week. On completing one project, they can pick up another base and work on additional features for their parks and cityscapes. Sometimes when the children decide to work together, I tell them, "You may wind up with one project. Then who will get it when it's done?" I want the children to know up front that they are going to have to deal with that question later on. They get into a long discussion about it. They may say to one another, "You can take it for one month and I'll take it for the next month." When they walk out of the room with both of them holding on to their construction, I never know how it will end up. I don't want to know. It's their business.

Sometimes, with the younger children, we construct "gardens" in the spring. I look around the room for things with different size openings, like plastic beads, shells, buttons. I also set out pipe cleaners and wires of various weights.

Instead of providing a base, I might just plunk down a piece of clay in front of them and simply insert a length of wire into it. (These are the stems on which the flowers and plants will be constructed.) I'll say to the children, "We're not going to model with this clay, but it will anchor a wire and that wire can support something else." I talk to them about twisting the wire to hold things as opposed to tying the wire. We talk about the various characteristics of flowers. The children might say, "Well, there's the flower, the stem, and maybe some leaves." (I might show them some catalogs of spring flowers that have just come out.) Then I'll say, "Maybe this big red button could be the flower, and how about a bit of ribbon for the leaf? You could twist a little something around."

Attaching various materials to construct a garden, Chelsea, age six, created an arrangement of stems, flowers, and leaves

Pretty soon, the children are twisting and joining and making flowers and plants for their little gardens. They are building things that grow and grow.

Note: Instead of using clay as the base, I sometimes provide chunks of Styrofoam into which the wires can be inserted. I'll also set out small, thin Styrofoam rectangles through which wires can be woven.

Papier-mâché

When the children are studying animals, we often use them as the subject for papier-mâché activities. To make the animal's body, we crumple up newspapers and bunch them together to create rounded shapes. Then we surround these shapes with a sheet of uncrumpled newspaper and tape it in place to hold it tight. Smaller sections are made in the same way for the head and legs. They are attached to the body with tape. Another way to make the body is to stuff a brown paper bag with crumpled newspapers or to use a long white paper bread bag, stuffing it all the way down to create a nice long shape.

A box can also serve as the animal's body. (If its shape is not quite right, some crumpled-up newspaper can be taped in place to create a more rounded look.) A smaller box might serve as the animal's head. If a suitable size isn't available, the head can be made with crumpled newspaper. For ears, noses, trunks, and tails, more newspaper is simply crumpled up and taped in place. At this point, the kids are consuming yards and yards of masking tape and I might be spending much of my time cutting as many more strips as they need.

The following week, we papier-mâché the animals. This process once called for a mix of flour and water, but we now use something called art paste, which is really good. It's a powdered concentrate that comes in a plastic bag set inside a small box. Stirred into a quantity of cold water for about three minutes, this powder produces a nice, clear gel-like goop. We actually call it goop. (You must follow the directions on the box, or else the mix will be lumpy.) After I pour some of this goop into a shallow aluminum cookie tray—which provides a wide, broad surface area—we dip strips of newspaper into it, shake off the excess, and wind the strips around the crumpled-newspaper animal. The papier-mâché process is sloppy. You can hear the kids saying to each other, "Oh, it's very yucky."

As the strips of papier-mâché are added, the animal may become heavy and begin to sag. To prevent this, I may gently turn it over so that the child can work on the other side. Or I may say, "It's getting too heavy. Let's put your animal on the shelf and we'll work on it next time."

By the following week, the papier-mâché has dried, forming a smooth, hard surface. The animals now have real form and personality. When the kids walk over to the shelf and pick them up, they reconnect with their work. Seeing their

When I asked nine-year-olds, "How can you construct a favorite animal?" they made them with cardboard boxes, newspaper, and papier-mâché. Sydney did a horse, Maya a giraffe. For Danny's camel, a can represented the hump

Five-year-old Lily constructed a figure and an animal in cardboard, adorned with fabric, yarn, and fur. These stick puppets are sometimes used in conjunction with such activities as block building

piece is a salutary experience; they're very satisfied and happy with themselves. They can now add the whiskers or whatever. (In a small box, I have little bits of corrugated cardboard that can serve as noses, ears, and tails.) The children can finish their pieces quite easily at this point by painting the animals with tempera. They use the same methods they learned in their painting class.

Stick Puppets

The five- and six-year-olds also get into figurative work by doing stick puppets. (These were once held up with sticks, but now a long, heavy strip of cardboard can be used to support them. I let the kids decide if they want to put them on a stick or not.) The puppets themselves are made of flat brown corrugated cardboard that has been precut into large and small rectangles. There are head sizes, body sizes, and leg sizes: a square head, a large rectangle for the body, and four skinny rectangles for the arms and legs.

To get the children started, I'll toss some of these pieces onto the table and say to one child, "How can you make a person or an animal out of these?" By moving the rectangles around, he or she finds a way. If the first child makes an animal, I'll ask another child, "How can you use the same shapes to make a person?" I show the children how to overlap the

A five-year-old child combined cardboard shapes, fur, felt, cotton, and beads to create this energetic cat

pieces slightly so they will hold together when glued. Then I invite them all to go to the boxes to get whatever they'll need to make a person or an animal. With their Elmer's glue, they can assemble an animal or a little human being in a short time.

Note: There are also times when I put out boxes with larger shapes that are not as clearly cut out as the rectangles, and I ask the kids to make an imaginary animal because there's a funny wing shape or some other sort of shape.

The stick puppets are a good example of work that does not fall neatly into a single art category, because they are somewhere between collage and construction. (They are also the precursors of the figurative work the kids will be doing later.) After they have made their puppets, I invite the children over to the collage boxes—sitting at the side of the room—to choose the pieces they think they will need for their animal or person. They can find yarn, felt, feathers, furs, fabrics, velvets, fake hair, and so on. By the time they've put a little hair on a rectangle and added two little beads or a button or whatever, they have created a face. The children sometimes ask about drawing or painting the face, but I say, "How can you do it with collage? Because that's what we're working with today."

Note: I'm a stickler for keeping the mediums separate. I find that if you mix them, the children won't try to find new possibilities or problem-solving methods for working with the different materials.

The children can hardly wait to get at the collage boxes. Then they get out their scissors and start cutting. They com-

This five-year-old girl is carefully cutting a shirt for her stick puppet to wear

plete their figures, investing a great deal of thought and effort in them. They are always amazed when their puppets come to life. Suddenly they have a person. They have made these clever little things by themselves and they are delighted by them. When they walk out of the room at the end of a forty-five-minute class, they have a little person in their hand.

Note: For the very young, letting them walk out of the room with their figures is a wonderful occasion. If I were to put them on display, the viewer would just gasp at the joy of looking at them. But it wouldn't be fair to the children not to let them take them home right away, because they get so much pleasure from them. (I've been told that the kids keep these stick puppets for years.)

For the eight- to ten-year-olds, we use paper fasteners to make the puppets jointed, so that parts of them can move.

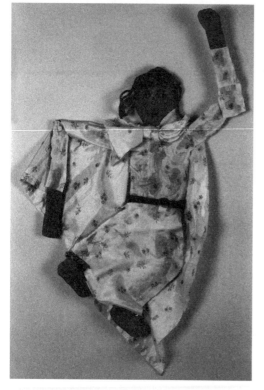

(ABOVE LEFT) *Ten-year-old Ruth created this stick puppet on skates. She used collage materials to show the long-sleeved dress and the pigtails*

(ABOVE RIGHT) *Nine-year-old Kristen did a portrait of herself as a stick puppet. She braided the yarn carefully to represent her hair*

(LEFT) *Ten-year-old Julia constructed a stick puppet as an Indian dancer with a flowing silk dress and bells on her ankles*

The other parts are glued together. I have an awl, which I push through to a board underneath, making a hole in the cardboard. The paper fastener, which is a brass disk with two pointed prongs attached to the back, easily goes straight through the hole. When the prongs are folded back, it holds the parts together but lets them move. The legs can move, the arms can move. I ask the children to bring me the pieces they want joined. They seem to want everything joined: arms, legs, knees, elbows. I limit them to one or two paper fasteners. I tell the kids, "You can have two. Choose which joints it will be." (Otherwise I would be joining those things all day.)

This girl, age ten, portrays herself as a dancer, using jointed cardboard to create the active figure

Working with the Figure

With the older children, we create other figures in three dimensions, using wires, newspaper, and masking tape. The newspaper, precut into sixteen-inch squares, is used to build up the forms by wrapping them diagonally around the wires. The masking tape holds the rolled newspaper in place. (The wires—green florist's wires—are eighteen inches long and come in twelve-pound boxes. Purchased from florists, they are identified as ASWG number 21. One of these boxes will last for years.)

The wire is bent at the ends to keep it from slipping out. The result is a long, skinny newspaper roll with a wire running through the middle. Every child gets three wires to serve as the armature for his or her figure.

Once the children make their armature rolls, we fold one in half for the legs, the other in half to become the head and torso, while the third goes through the body to represent the arms. The head and the torso can be filled out with a bit of newspaper, bunched together and taped in place.

These figures are usually shown in action. Because the armature is extremely flexible, the children can easily bend the torso, arms, legs, knees, and elbows to create any kind of action figure they want. They can quickly make a figure in motion. Who that person will be is completely up to the child. It might be a famous baseball player, an ice skater, or a basketball player who is leaping up to dunk the ball into the basket. The figures the kids make are amazing, and making them is exciting for the kids. It's about as good as it gets.

The children may put two figures together, such as a hockey player with a stick and a goalie at the net. Sometimes there may be three different action figures on one base. We may then draw these in charcoal. (It's a wonderful way to get some figure drawing going from the kids' own little armature figures.)

The following week the children paint the skin and give their figures faces and hair. They endow them with real personality. The children are completely connected to their creations. Every time they work with these figures, they are looking into the face of a little human being.

The children dress their figures with materials from the collage boxes. I don't set these boxes out on a table, but the kids know they can poke their heads into them, hunt about, and pull things out that might work for them. They can dress their action figures any way they like, plain or fancy.

We also do armature figures from history, about ten to twelve inches high, that are related to their social studies curriculum. These, of course, require authentic costumes. We study the period involved. We research the costumes with the help of the classroom teacher. We read books on the subject and look at reproductions of paintings from the period. We get out the scraps of fabric to find the satins and silks, furs and leathers, whatever might be needed. Then we correct the costume to make sure it's authentic. These little figures become important elements in the children's social studies learning.

FOR PARENTS

Parents who'd like their kids to do construction at home have asked:

Isn't construction a bit too complicated to tackle?
Not really. Construction can take place anywhere. Just give the kids some boxes, a pair of scissors, a roll of tape, and a big

sheet of cardboard to build on and they'll be very clever about putting them all together.

Isn't construction similar to block building?
It's as engaging as block building, and a whole world can be developed with these things. The children can join and glue the boxes together. They can cut the paper towel tubes into rings that serve as wheels for a car.

What about the work space needed?
Well, that's the key. Where you live will determine the scale of the work. People living in big houses can save lots of boxes and paper tubes and containers and use an attic or an en-closed porch as the work area. Several children can crowd around there and build a whole city with these boxes. And pretty soon, you have the fire station, the police station, the bakery, and vehicles in the streets.

What about the children who live in small apartments?
Parents there can collect the small-scale stuff. They can put a bag on the doorknob of their kitchen and collect spaghetti boxes and the cardboard tubes that come with paper towels and toilet tissue along with a bunch of smaller boxes, like those for toothpaste. When it's a rainy day and the kids are stuck at home, the parents can set a pile of these tubes and boxes on the kitchen table and the children can go to work, putting them together and gluing them.

What about painting the finished constructions?
They don't have to be painted. The children can put colored paper on them or glue on some fabrics, textures, etcetera. The

finished work may not look razzle-dazzle because the kids are not into that. If they do want to paint the work, they can use acrylics.

What about including figures of people?
The children can populate their cities with stick puppets, papier-mâché figures, or wire armature figures. The simple cardboard stick puppets can be anchored in place with Velcro. The papier-mâché and wire armature figures can stand up on their own. Such figures are not always something the kids can do independently, so you can help here. For the papier-mâché figures, newspaper is bunched up to make the forms and held together with tape, then covered with strips of newspaper dipped in a flour-and-water mixture or an art paste (as was described earlier in this chapter). When dry, these figures become nice and sturdy. For the armature figures, the wire can come from various sources, such as discards from rewiring jobs. It's the perfect material for doing figures, so if you come by some in the street, grab it.

What if the kids are not very ambitious?
It isn't necessary to do a whole city. In my classes, I see boys who spend their whole time creating a perfect vehicle. One child—using tubes and boxes—did a plane that was really elegant. He mounted it on three supports that were wooden coffee stirrers. I could see the child taking the next step at home, painting his plane in acrylic with great care and love and perhaps adding the letters USA or NASA on the wings or the sides.

You talk about the importance of saving the children's work. What about the clutter here?

With big constructions, it's the process of putting them together that counts. And you will soon throw them away. This is part of childhood. This is part of life. You don't want to sit around and look at those cereal boxes forever. They may represent a bakery to your child, but they're still cereal boxes to you.

SOCIAL STUDIES

Social Studies teaches how various people live together in their societies, the rules they make for themselves, and how they adapt to their particular geography and climate. Art makes these social studies even more alive and serves as the springboard for many activities as well. Through art, the children can re-create real and imagined environments and experience what it's like to live in another culture. The children can also study the artifacts and art objects of other cultures, not to replicate them but to understand their purpose. While working in the style of a culture, the children can at the same time draw on their personal experiences, making these objects their own.

For example, we made some Greek vases in clay. The vases originally had depicted Greek games, but we transposed the theme to the sports that children typically play today. We re-created the vases in the style of ancient Greece, but the images the children painted on them came from their own active involvement with baseball, basketball, and other sports.

Although I have largely targeted the children's personal lives as subject matter in the art room, I often turn to social studies for additional ideas and imagery. In our school, social studies is the core curriculum around which almost everything revolves. Since this represents a large part of the children's daily life, they usually develop a strong sense of identification with the subject. So I always keep closely in touch with what the kids are studying in their classrooms. When I have lunch with the other teachers, I learn what they are doing. When I hear that they are exploring a certain culture, I seek out examples of its art, trying to find out why it was done, how it was done, and what it says about its people.

Note: Classroom teachers, being more familiar with the subject, can introduce certain art activities themselves, encouraging the children to re-create the environments or study the artifacts of other cultures.

In social studies, as elsewhere, different age groups respond differently. Five-, six-, and seven-year-olds are quite involved in the here and now. By seven and eight, they are able to understand the past history of their localities as well. By nine and ten, they are ready to tackle far distant lands and ancient cultures. (They can also render complex narratives with great elaboration and rich detail.)

Taking Trips
The youngest children study their immediate community by taking trips to a local bakery, fire station, farm, or orchard. The class discussion that follows can lead to various art activ-

ities, such as the painting of murals or the making of models to show the environments in miniature. Discussion is the key to helping the children organize these activities. You ask them, "Where did we go?" "What did we see?" (You may write the children's replies on the blackboard.) The kids remember what they saw. They talk about what they did.

After a trip to the orchard, for example, you might ask, "Were the trees in a line or were they scattered about?" The kids will reply, "The trees were planted in rows." You might ask, "What was on the tree?" The kids will say, "There were green apples and red apples." The children will also remember that a stand selling apples and pumpkins was next to the orchard. They may also recall that the day was cold and that they were wearing woolen scarves. You might then ask, "How can you show me this experience on a very large piece of paper?" Or, "How can you do a painting of the trip we took to the orchard?"

Then you have the children push some tables together in the room or have them work outside in the hall. You roll out some brown mural paper, perhaps three feet wide and about six feet long. You also set some paints out on a tray, which several kids can share. The children then begin work on their mural. Sometimes they predraw their images with chalk before painting them. (Between sessions, the mural paper is rolled up.)

Young children need a clear baseline (a street or a skyline) to make sense of their mural. It's confusing for them to try to orient themselves in space. When the paper is on the floor and they're gathered around, they might draw an image that appears to be upside down when the mural is hung on the wall. This situation can stimulate a class discussion about how things look in space. It offers an opportunity for the children to share their understanding of what's going on and to learn from one another.

The children plan and paint their murals, working in groups of five or six. If the group is large, half of the kids can be doing the painting while the other half works on stick puppets. (They can choose or draw straws for these assignments.) The stick puppets can be attached to the mural with bits of Velcro; they can also be moved about.

The children who visited the orchard made little stick puppets of themselves wearing scarves. Their teacher appeared as a stick puppet as well. The mural also included the bus that took the class to the orchard, along with its driver. Working on the mural was a concrete way for the kids to say, "I've had this experience and I understand what I did."

Note: When a mural is finished, it may be hung on the main wall of the classroom, or in the hallway, or on a staircase. (After a time, when it has served its purpose, the mural is taken down.)

If the class went to a farm, you might ask, "What do you remember about our trip?" The children may reply, "There was a barn." "There was a place for the chickens." "We saw where they milked the cows." You may then suggest that the children make a model of the farm rather than a mural. You might say, "You can put the land for the farm on a table and put the buildings and the animals and the people that you make right on top of it."

If the seven- and eight-year-olds are studying Native Americans, you might ask, "How can you paint a mural that will tell how the Lanape Indians lived?" The children can be

After a trip to the Statue of Liberty, nine-year-old Genevieve painted the strong shape of the figure on its solid pedestal (18″ × 24″). I noted this, then said, "Her face and red lips give me the feeling that you really liked her"

given a list of Indian names and asked to choose names for themselves. You then say, "It's now morning [or afternoon or evening]. How can you show us something about your life at this time?" Or, "What is it like to be living in your village?" The children may then depict the Indians going fishing, playing games, and so forth, based on their classroom study. Or you might ask one group of kids, "How would the Lanape Indians live in the winter?" And ask another group, "How would they live in the summer?" The seasonal variations could serve as the theme for two separate murals.

One year, the eight- and nine-year-olds did murals that compared and contrasted the Colonial settlements of Plymouth and Williamsburg. The Plymouth mural depicted bumpy little hills by the sea. The Williamsburg mural showed a wide main street lined with magnificent houses. After they had established these basic and distinguishing features, the children painted in the details. As they worked, they had their differences, as in deciding where the town hall should go. But, in the end, the kids worked out all these problems.

Although art activities provide the opportunity for a great learning and sharing experience, many classroom teachers believe they should occur at the end of the learning process. They think that a mural or a model should be created after the children have already studied the culture. But if these activities are introduced somewhat earlier—as the kids are getting into their studies—the art experience can become another way for them to research and learn about their subject.

Other Projects

One group of nine- and ten-year-olds who were studying Colonial America were reading a wonderful book, Gary Bowen's

Stranded at Plimoth Plantation 1626, published by Harper-Collins in 1994. The book tells of a boy who was an indentured servant, but who had the option of leaving when he came of age. By that time he had fallen so much in love with the people of Plymouth that he stayed on. The book's illustrations are a series of beautiful woodcuts that depict Colonial life in terms of, among other things, objects in the house, food, animals, and activities in the larger community.

I asked the children to think about these categories in their own lives and to make linoleum prints of them so that we might put a book together about contemporary life. I asked them, "What are the foods you eat?" "What are the things you have in your house?" "What kind of animals do you have?" So the children did these images of their own lives. Each was to contribute one print, but they made enough copies so that they could share them with each other. All the children then had a complete set of prints, which they assembled into little books for themselves.

Another group of nine- and ten-year-olds, studying the early Plymouth settlement, learned about Paperotamia, an art form involving cut paper. Because paper was so scarce and valuable in those days, the colonists treasured it and used it in making decorative cutouts. The children were challenged to see what they could do in the same situation. They were restricted to a single piece of paper—as opposed to collage, where they could always have as much paper as they wanted.

Like the colonists, the children made their cutout designs by first folding their single sheet of paper in half. They knew how to do hearts, and tried out many heart ideas that way. One boy who liked frogs tried cutting one out, and it appeared doubled and was fascinating to look at. When the children were done, they mounted their cutouts on another piece of paper and framed them. They found this project very satisfying and the results were glorious.

A class of eight- and nine-year-olds was given embroidery hoops and little pieces of linen to do Colonial embroidery. I taught them the cross-stitch, which is the basic stitch of samplers, and had them stitch their own names or those of their pets. Once they mastered the cross-stitch, they learned other stitches for the borders. Since only girls did embroidery in Colonial times, the boys took girls' names (William, for example, became Wilhelmina). The children carried their samplers with them wherever they went: to the gym, to the yard. The sight of nine-year-old boys walking down the hallways of our school doing embroidery was really something to see.

The seven- and eight-year-olds have also made Dutch dolls using newspaper-and-wire armature figures and dressing them in the style of the 1640s. We've also made Dutch dolls as stick puppets and have similarly created Hindu as well as Native American figures.

A group of seven- and eight-year-olds was studying New Amsterdam. The children were learning about the Dutch immigrants who came to Manhattan island and the indigenous people they found already there when they arrived, along with such local animals as deer and porcupine. To tell their story, the children combined Styrofoam prints and collage. (For social studies activities I sometimes mix the media.) The collage depicted various scenes and landscapes. Some children cut out of paper the Dutch houses with their stepped roofs and divided doors. Some created a woodsy scene with a creek running through it.

The Styrofoam prints were used to produce multiple people and animals that would populate these scenes. The children then cut these out in silhouette. For a landscape, one child might use the print cutouts of Native Americans with their bows and arrows and maybe a deer or two. Another child might show animals going down to the water to drink in a woodsy landscape. The kids traded their Styrofoam prints with each other, so that those who needed more people or more animals could have them.

The nine- and ten-year-olds studying Africa were reading folk tales about animals. In the school's wood shop, they had been making wood blocks of these animals, involving pieces of pine and metal tools. (The idea was to combine these prints as a bestiary of African animals.) I thought it might be stimulating to pick up on this theme as a collage by asking the kids how they could cut the same animals out of paper. I also encouraged them to elaborate further by repeating simple geometric designs in the African style because there are many patternings in African art. I showed them examples of some of the wonderful repeats used on African fabrics printed with indigo dye, such as Adinkra and Adire Eleko cloths, deriving, respectively, from Ghana and Nigeria.

We have also re-created the pottery and related motifs of cultures other than the Greek. When the children were studying Native Americans, we made an outdoor kiln in the schoolyard using a big garbage can and sawdust. The pots were burnished when they were almost dry by rubbing them with a smooth stone to make them shiny. When burnished and dry, the pots were fired in our kiln. The oxidation of the burning sawdust turned them black. We had a great time doing this because it seemed so authentic. (However, I was asked to discontinue the activity because of the strong smells the process was generating.)

*Katie, age ten,
depicted an elephant
in her African
animal collage,
surrounded by a
patterned border
(11″ × 12″)*

*Ben, age ten, did a
collage of African
animals showing
tigers, surrounded by
a patterned border
(11″ × 12″)*

Clay mugs made by eight-year-olds using the slab method. These were incised with scenes of Arctic life

We've also made Ming vases with the nine- and ten-year-olds. In the seventeenth century, the Chinese codified many of their brushwork motifs. I asked each child to memorize one motif that could be used on his on her own pottery. They were to learn how to draw the leaf and stalk of the bamboo plant or a certain flower. (The idea was to draw the motif without having it in front of them.) I provided catalogs of trees, plants, and flowers, then let each child pick a page and choose a motif to memorize. I told them that if they were going to do a flower, they should study the outer rim of the petals the first night, the inner rim of the petals the second night, the center of the flower the third night, and so on until the class met again the following week.

Some children were panicked and insisted that they couldn't memorize it. Of course, these were the kids who knew exactly how to do it the following week. They seemed to love the challenge. When it was time to glaze their vases, I asked the children, "How can you include the motif that you

A collographic plate and its print in white ink on black paper made by Lily and Lena, both age nine, depicts an Arctic scene (14" × 23"). They cut the shapes from flat and corrugated cardboard, made several prints, then shared them

studied?" So they drew their chrysanthemums or their daffodils or whatever, and these appeared as a blue glaze on a white background.

When the nine- and ten-year-olds were studying various aspects of the Middle Ages in England, they also learned about trade routes in the Middle East and about Arabic culture. We went to the Metropolitan Museum of Art and looked at the incredible tile work that came out of that culture.

At the time, the children were writing poetry, so they used that idea for their tiles. They carved an image from their own poetry (or from the poem of a famous poet) in the center. Then, because the Arabs do calligraphy, the children chose some simple words from their poem and wrote them in glaze on the outer edge of the tile. (They had to keep the writing simple because the tiles were small.)

Their tiles were glazed in turquoise, cobalt blue, and white, which are typical Middle Eastern colors. Each tile represented a combination of the child's own poetry, his carved relief, and his glazes; it was all individualized and personal. We also did a decorative arch over a doorway in our school, made of interlocking larger Arabic tiles and including various words to describe our school's attributes. These words were written in a beautiful calligraphy.

Another time we did two huge mosaics, using tiles with many gradations in color—each no bigger than half an inch square—that we made ourselves. One involved the Greek myth of Ceres and Persephone in the underworld. The

After a social studies–related museum trip, nine- and ten-year-olds used the clay slab method to create burial pottery in the style of the Han Dynasty. Drew made a watch tower with a moon window and Dylan put a dragon on his roof, while Kristen modeled some farm animals

other, set near the World Trade Center, had a man with his briefcase going down the steps of the subway, headed into that underground system. The shapes and colors of the mosaics were lively. Both scenes were mounted on plywood panels and now stand on either side of the stage in our auditorium.

One year, a group of nine- and ten-year-olds were studying India. I went to the art museum and researched Hindu

Olivia, age ten, worked in the style of Persian miniatures to paint an elephant near water. She used tempera, silver and gold paint, and a tiny brush for her elaborate patterning, then mounted the painting on a sheet of marble paper she made herself (12″ × 16″)

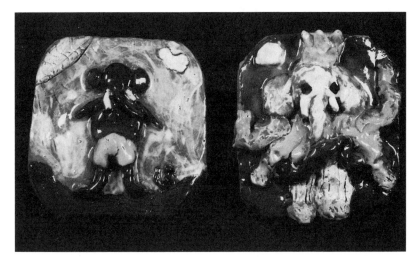

Clay relief sculptures, fired and glazed, of the god Ganesha, made by ten-year-olds learning about India in social studies

paintings and sculptures, then showed the children photographs of Hindu art, characterized in part by wonderful large, frontal eyes set in profiled heads. After we looked at these and talked about the attributes of Hindu art, I asked the children to do themselves in profile in the form of little clay bas-reliefs that showed them doing something active over the summer.

Our most ambitious project involved creating Hindu "temples" in clay. We began by studying photographs of such temples with their highly ornamented sides and their intricately carved reliefs. Each child then researched the country's flora and fauna, made a sketch of one example, then transferred it to a slab of clay as a Hindu-style bas-relief.

Four kids were involved with creating each temple. Each child did a façade. Five pieces were required: the four sides and the top. (Those who finished early did the finial that would sit on top.) After the pieces came out of the kiln, we wired them together. (We had made small holes in the sides so that they could be hooked up together to create one large temple.) To give the work a solid center, we used gallon-sized Clorox containers, stood upright, around and over which the clay slabs or façades were arranged. Those temples were impressive; even somewhat awesome.

We also studied Persian carpet designs because of the Islamic influence on Hindu art, and saw how the patterns, borders, and floral motifs were repeated. We talked about what a repeat meant, that if a curved shape extends from the right side of one rose, it has to extend from the right side of every rose.

Each child then made his or her own "carpet," prepainting the borders and central motif on a large sheet of paper in rich red, gold, and rose (the basic colors of Persian carpets). Then I gave them a homework assignment to take home photocopies of Persian carpet patterns and memorize two flowers from them, then come back and make two kinds of stamps from them in class, which they would use to stamp around the edges of their own carpets. Soon the children were stamping gold roses, and stamping a green leaf between each rose, and maybe some chrysanthemums across the center. At the end, they went to a table where there were tiny brushes and other colors. Then they painted in all kinds of other repeats to finish up their carpets.

Another group of nine- and ten-year-olds, who were studying ancient Egypt, painted a mural that showed people presenting gifts to the pharaoh. Illustrated here was the life in the pharaoh's court, including the dancers and the river Nile, with ducks swimming in it. After studying Egyptian wall paintings, the children drew the figures as the Egyptians did, with frontal bodies and the heads in profile, and large single eyes that seemed to be looking in all directions.

This work was done in their classroom. At the same time, other children were creating small three-dimensional displays based on such Egyptian themes as medicine, music, and child care. (The kids had written research papers on these.) Two children were assigned to each model and developed it, using cardboard, plasticine, paint, and fabric. (The model on medicine showed a man being cured with a poultice.)

A class of eight- and nine-year-olds did a three-dimensional model of an Arctic scene, creating a little Eskimo village. The children began with a flat piece of plywood. They bunched up newspapers for the land forms, then covered them with plaster and built up the rest of the village on top. (The igloos were also made of the white plaster of Paris.) The

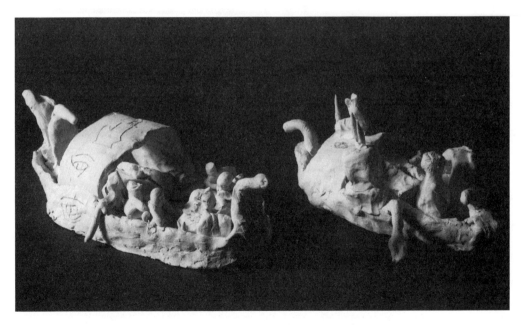

When I asked nine- and ten-year-olds, studying ancient Egypt, what they would take with them on a barque journeying to the Land of the Dead, one girl took her friends. The other took her cat, and her TV set

Students of all ages participated in painting this large outdoor mural in the school yard, depicting lower Manhattan and the bay. Everyone was pleased with the results

model showed some Inuits standing near holes in the ice, with their spears at the ready. They were waiting for the seals to emerge.

When the kids were doing their murals, they would sometimes skip lunch to work on them. They loved their murals and wanted to give them as much time as they could. When the children who were working on the Arctic village would arrive in the morning (and almost before they took off their backpacks), they would crowd around their model. It was as though they were living in this miniature world, connecting with it emotionally and somehow integrating its feelings and meanings into their own lives. Such memories may linger long after the school year ends. If you ask adults what they recall about their classroom activities, the group art they did for social studies is quite often the experience they remember most vividly.

Museum Trips

Museum trips can be a wonderful learning experience for children. It is important that they see real work whenever possible—work that artists have actually made as opposed to looking only at reproductions. The children can then see the richness of the colors, the quality of the paint, the texture of a surface. If the work is three-dimensional, they can walk around it. (For teachers of social studies in particular, it is important to visit museums and exhibitions that are relevant to their curriculum activities.)

Before the trip, the teacher should visit the exhibition and select a few works that the children might study in depth. It's also useful to prepare a "trip sheet" in advance. This consists of a series of instructions on where to go in the exhibit and what to observe. The trip sheet might also list a number of questions to ask the children. These should be kept simple, such as:

- What do you notice here?
- What is this piece made of?
- What is the artist's idea and how does he show it?

Rather than tell the kids what they are seeing, it's best to let them look at and discover the works for themselves. The art will unfold for them as they do so.

Along with the trip sheet, also take some paper and pencils. Then, near the end of the visit, ask the kids to choose their favorite work and draw it. This will help the children develop their observational skills. The drawings can also enhance class discussions after the kids return from their museum trip.

Note: These ideas can easily be adapted by parents who have access to museums and to art exhibitions.

CONCLUSION

Teaching art to children calls for a good deal of preparation. To make it all work, you have to scrounge for materials, think ahead, plan ahead, and set things up in advance.

If I have set out the materials clearly in my classes, and asked relevant questions, then I can trust the children to like art and to produce meaningful results. They have demonstrated this over and over again. I trust them completely. They are honest about their responses and they care about what they do.

It is difficult to make any judgments about one's effect on children. You get the kids who say, "I'm going to be an artist when I grow up." If one child makes that announcement, then of course many others are going to be artists too. I say, "That's a very important thing to be." And we leave it at that. I am particularly touched by children who say they are going to be art teachers when they grow up. Few of the children I teach will eventually become artists or even art teachers, but I believe they all deserve a warm and encouraging access to this splendid visual language we call art.

Index of Activities by Age Group

Bibliography

Some of the books listed here, although out of print, are included because they're worth seeking out from library sources.

Burton, Judith M. A series of six articles on "Developing Minds," *School Arts* magazine (1980, 1981). Covering the variety of learning experiences that working with art provides for children, these articles look at the way that theory and practice are integrated in art teaching.

Churchill, Angiola R. *Art for Preadolescents*. New York: McGraw-Hill, 1970. This book addresses with wisdom the often overlooked and sometimes difficult preadolescent age group, nine- to thirteen-year-olds. Dealing with group behavior and suitable subject matter, it also includes information on art history and criticism.

D'Amico, Victor, and Arlette Buchman. *Assemblage: A New Dimension in Creative Teaching in Action*. New York: Museum of Modern Art, 1972. Based on classes given at the Museum of Modern Art in New York, this book includes hundreds of actual lessons together with specific materials and discussions for each. It's richly illustrated, with examples of work by museum artists and the students themselves.

Ewing, Patrick, with Linda L. Louis. *In the Paint*. New York: Abbeville Kids Press, 1999. An exploration of how to paint with children, especially in a home setting.

Lord, Lois. *Collage and Construction in School: Preschool–Junior High School*. Worcester, Mass: Davis Publications, 1958; New York: Bank Street College of

Education, 1996. An in-depth approach to collage and construction for children of various ages. Based on a keen understanding of the child's developmental growth, this book offers a wealth of excellent suggestions on materials and motivations.

Lowenfeld, Viktor, and W. Lambert Brittain. *Creative and Mental Growth*. New York: Macmillan, 1947. (The eighth edition was published in 1987.) A classic in its field, republished many times, this book puts children at the center of the art experience and covers a particularly wide selection of ages, ranging from two to seventeen.

Nager, Nancy, and Edna K. Shapiro. *Revisiting a Progressive Pedagogy: The Developmental-Interaction Approach*. Albany: State University of New York Press, 2000. A thoughtful book that looks at what has happened to progressive education, with particular attention to the developmental-interactive approach associated with the Bank Street School for Children. Its excellent chapter on art education presents a close look at the social lessons that occur through the art experiences of children.

Pile, Naomi. *Art Experiences for Young Children*. New York: Macmillan, 1973. This book focuses on the exploration and process of art, not on producing a specific product. It is a sensitive, child-centered guide to appropriate art experiences for young children from the ages of three to six.

Schuman, Jo Miles. *Art from Many Hands: Multicultural Art Projects*. Worcester, Mass.: Davis Publications, 1981. An essential book for those who teach social studies–related art. Covering authentic cultural activities, it shows how world art can serve as a springboard for personal expression rather than as something merely to copy.

Silberstein-Storfer, Muriel. *Doing Art Together*. New York: Simon & Schuster, 1982. This book describes parents and children appreciating and creating art together at the Parent-Child Workshop at the Metropolitan Museum of Art in New York.

Smith, Nancy. *Experience and Art: Teaching Children to Paint*. New York: Teachers College Press, 1983, 1993. The single most valuable study of children's painting and the process by which they can be helped to paint. A "must" for art teachers, it is based on how children grow, think, learn, and express themselves. The book also includes motivational questions for all age levels.

Smith, Nancy, and the Drawing Study Group. *Observation Drawing with Children*. New York: Teachers College Press, 1998. A wonderful guide that helps teachers approach observational drawing in ways that invite children to see and to express themselves with individuality.